AIDS TO DEVOTION

AIDS TO DEVOTION

THOUGHTS ON THE HOLY SPIRIT
IN THE EPISTLE TO THE EPHESIANS

ANDREW MURRAY

Lakeland
Marshall Morgan & Scott
3 Beggarwood Lane, Basingstoke,
Hants RG23 7LP, UK

First published by Lakeland
This edition issued in 1985 by
Marshall Pickering Communications Ltd

British Library Cataloguing in Publication Data

Murray, Andrew, *1828-1917*
    Aids to devotion.
    1. Devotional literature
    I. Title
    242   BV832.2

ISBN 0 551 00241 7

Printed and bound in Great Britain by
Anchor Brendon Ltd, Tiptree, Essex

PREFACE

SOME years ago I was asked to write a series of articles under the heading, "AIDS TO DEVOTION," for the *Lovedale Christian Express*. My mind was at the time much occupied with the Epistle to the Ephesians, and I thought it might be possible to connect its teaching with the effort to give some help for the Quiet Hour. This led to my writing two of the introductory chapters, and the twelve that deal with the chief thoughts of the Epistle.

I am deeply conscious of how defective they are and how little able I have been to satisfy myself in giving expression to what I think I have seen of the treasures that God has stored away in this Epistle for His Church. I have nevertheless ventured on their publication in this little booklet, in the hope that God may use them to help some of His children to realise what the standard of the true Christian life is as it is set before us in the Epistle, and what absolute divine assurance it gives us that God is able and willing to make all that it contains true in our experience.

I send this little book out with the prayer with which Paul wrote his Epistle, "that God, the Father of glory may give you the Spirit of wisdom and revelation in the knowledge of Himself." Without that Spirit, specially sought, and received, and yielded to in great teachableness, the truths of the Epistle will remain a hidden mystery. With that teaching, we shall "be filled with the knowledge of God's Will in all wisdom and spiritual understanding," we shall learn to know what passeth knowledge, and be brought to experience that His power is able actually to do in us exceeding abundantly above what we can ask or think.

ANDREW MURRAY

CONTENTS

INTRODUCTION

I

DEVOTION IN SECRET PRAYER AND IN DAILY LIFE

"Pray to thy Father which is in secret, and thy Father shall reward thee openly."—MATT. vi. 6.

WE use the word devotion in two senses. First, with regard to prayer in our public and private devotions. Then with regard to that spirit of devotion, or devotedness to God, which is to mark our daily life. We have the two thoughts in our text. If in the inner chamber we truly meet our Father who seeth in secret, He will give us the open reward of grace to live our life to His glory, the entire and continual devotion of our whole being to His will. THE ACT OF DEVOTION secures the power for THAT SPIRIT OF DEVOTION which is to pervade our daily life to His glory.

The classic passage on the law of devotion we find in Lev. xxvii. 28. "No devoted thing that a man shall devote unto the Lord, shall be sold or redeemed; EVERY DEVOTED THING IS MOST HOLY UNTO THE LORD." The solemn story of Achan is the best commentary on the words (Joshua vi. 17, 18; vii. 11, R.V.). "The city shall be devoted." "And, ye, in any wise, keep yourselves from the devoted thing, lest when ye have devoted it, ye take of the devoted thing; so shall ye make the camp of Israel accursed." The punishment, first on Israel in its defeat, and then on Achan, gave a solemn illustration of how real the meaning of devotion is in God's sight. DEVOTION IS THE WHOLE-HEARTED AND IRREVOCABLE GIVING UP TO GOD OF WHAT MAY NEVER BE TAKEN BACK AGAIN. The person or thing is ''MOST HOLY TO THE LORD''.

Aids to devotion may be given in more than one way. The simplest would be to suggest what is helpful in our time of retirement to prepare us for worshipping God in truth. We might take up some of the chief hindrances from which our devotions suffer, or some of the reasons that these hindrances have such power over us, or some of the helps that could enable us to pray more nearly as Scripture enjoins. In a little book, like Dr. Moule's *Secret Prayer*, one finds beautiful and most helpful thoughts, supplying just what is needed in this direction. Another way might be to seek by a series of Scripture meditations so to encourage desire and strengthen faith as to waken in the reader the sentiment which can make his devotions a joy to himself, and give him the humble trust that they are pleasing to God. A book, for instance, like Bowen's *Daily Meditations*, or Spurgeon's *Day Book*, has been found helpful to multitudes.

But there is still another way which, though more difficult, has its advantages. It does not deal directly with the act of devotion, but with that spirit and temper which is to rule us all the day, and fill the actions of our common life with true devotion to God. The chief object would be to rouse the personal activity of the worshipper, stirring him to inquiry as to what he truly regards as the meaning of a life wholly given up to God, His will, and His glory; as to the thought he has of the extent to which it is absolutely obligatory and attainable; as to what he thinks of his attainments or failures in the past and their causes; and as to the measure of effort and self-denial which he counts needful to succeed in the pursuit.

In education we are constantly told that the chief rule in all teaching is this:—the mind of the pupil is to be wakened and stimulated to self-activity. It is only when you have roused within him the consciousness of his powers, and have led him on to taste the joy of victory over apparently insurmountable difficulties, that you really give him the key by which he can discover truths for himself. No one can do us a greater favour than by stimulating thought and desire, rousing us to throw our whole energy into the work of training ourselves to seek with our whole heart such a spirit of life and devotion as shall be most pleasing to God.

Socrates has been called the greatest teacher (after Christ) the world has ever seen. He communicated no knowledge; he simply asked questions, and helped his scholars, first to see their own ignorance, then to know their powers of thought and reason, and then to understand that the real value of knowledge lay in its moral power, as the truth was received in the heart and the life. More than one humble and thoughtful inquirer owed to him the unfolding of all that was meant in his words, Know thyself.

In these days in which men profess to have little time for retirement and personal meditation on divine truth, we might well long for a Socrates to rouse us by his questions, to find out whether we really understand the words we use, and believe the truths we profess. The heathen Socrates might teach many a Christian what the meaning is of true religion, and give him most helpful aid in his devotion. Of all our religious writers there is none so much like Socrates, in his method of teaching, as William Law. In his deep sense of the unreality of our traditional belief, in his exposure of the inconsistency between a faithful observance of our public or private devotions, and a life devoted to the world, he seeks to make us know ourselves, both in our ignorance and in the powers that slumber in us. And just as Socrates always appealed to the divine voice within him, "that a god had ordered him to spend his life in proving to himself and others whether we are giving ourselves to right living," so Law, especially in his later writings, ever aims to rouse the faith that Christ dwells in the heart, and that in all our ignorance and impotence we may count upon the aid of His life and Spirit.

A few words from the first chapter of Law's *Serious Call*, on the nature of Christian devotion, will illustrate this. "There is not a shadow of a reason why we should in our prayers look wholly to God, and pray according to His will, but what equally proves it necessary for us to look wholly to God, and make His will and His glory the rule of our daily life." . . . "There is no reason why our prayers should be wise and holy and heavenly, but that our lives may be of the same nature, and that we may live to God in the same spirit that we pray to Him."

The one lesson is: our lives must be as holy as our prayers. Our prayers are to prove their reality by the fruit they bear in the holiness of our life. True devotion in prayer will assuredly be rewarded, by God's grace, with the power to live a life of true devotion to Him and His service. "Pray to thy Father in secret, and thy Father will reward thee openly."

Let Socrates, let William Law, let our own heart and conscience enforce the questions which these thoughts suggest. Or rather, let Jesus Christ Himself, our blessed Teacher, guide us to find out whether our devotion is such as He asks, a full surrender to God in secret every day, and a full devotion to His glory all the day.

II

DEVOTION—THE NEW TESTAMENT STANDARD

"Howbeit for this cause I obtained mercy, that in me as chief might Jesus Christ show forth all His long-suffering, for an ensample of them which should hereafter believe on Him."—1 TIM. i. 16.

IN any judgment we pronounce, everything depends upon the standard by which we measure. To those who are content with the level of our ordinary Christianity, though they may acknowledge that their own devotion is most defective, there will yet be no deep conviction of its sinfulness, or of the need and the possibility of any higher attainment. But when once we begin to see what really is the standard of the New Testament, and its universal obligation, we shall feel how far we come short of it. And we shall be convicted of the great sin of unbelief in the power of Jesus to keep us from sin and to enable us to walk so as to please God. And we shall find in God's Word that however impossible the standard is with men, it is not impossible with God, Who worketh in us to will and to do by the power of His Holy Spirit.

To discover what is really the New Testament standard of devotion is not an easy matter. Our preconceived opinions blind us; our environment exercises a powerful influence. Unless there be a very sincere desire truly to know the whole will of God, and a very prayerful dependence on the Holy Spirit's teaching, we may search in vain. But let everyone who is truly willing to live entirely for God, and desires in everything to please Him, be of good courage: God means us to know His will, and has promised by the Spirit to reveal it to us.

Paul tells us that Christ made him an ensample to all believers, and frequently admonishes the churches to follow his example (1 Cor. iv. 16; 1 Cor. xi. 1; Phil. iii. 17, iv. 9; 1 Thess. i. 6; 2 Thess. iii. 9). In studying what the true type of New Testament devotion is we cannot do better than take Paul as a pattern. The question might be asked, why, when God had given His Son as our perfect pattern, Paul should also be needed? The answer is of deep importance. Many look upon Christ in His sinless perfection as so utterly beyond what we can attain, that His example loses much of its force. But in Paul, the chief of sinners, we feel that there is here a man of like passions with ourselves. In him Christ gave proof, for all time, of what He could do for a sinner in saving and keeping from sin. What Christ has done for him, He can and will do for us too. If Christians would but make a careful study of the life of devotion which Christ enabled Paul to live, we should be one step nearer the time when absolute and entire devotion to God, as set before us in Scripture, should be counted essential to a true Christian life.

Someone may ask, how there should be such a difference between the standard in our churches and that of the New Testament. Do not our creeds give God's Word the place of honour, and acknowledge Scripture as our only guide? A little reflection will suggest the answer. Not long after the first generations of Christians had passed away, terrible corruptions entered into the Church, so that in course of time the Church sank into the darkness of the Middle Ages. With the Reformation and the preaching of Justification by Faith there was indeed a great revival of Christian truth, but without the corresponding revival of Christian life and practice. When the Bohemian Brethren, followers of John Huss, whose church order for the spiritual care of their members proved how doctrine and life were indissolubly linked together, sent deputations to the Reformers, Calvin wrote in answer that he congratulated them that, in addition to pure doctrine, they maintained such good discipline and morals. And he adds, "We have long since recognised the value of such a system, but cannot in any way attain to it." And Bucer wrote, "You alone in the whole world combine a wholesome discipline with pure faith. When we compare our church with yours, we must be ashamed."

While we bless God for the Reformation, we must never forget THAT IT WAS NOT PENTECOST. The spirit and power of Pentecost was something infinitely greater. Church history tells us that in the early ages of the Church it sometimes took half a century and more before some of the great doctrines of our creed were fully understood and formulated. It was not given to one generation to develop more than one truth at a time. And so it was at the Reformation too. It needed all the strength of the Reformers to free the great doctrine of Justification by Faith from the errors under which it had been buried. The full exposition of the doctrine of Sanctification, of the power and work of the Holy Spirit, of the calling of the Church to preach the Gospel to the heathen,—these truths were left to later ages. And even now in studying so momentous a question as the true standard of spiritual devotion to God, we must beware of not looking to the Reformation, or to later ages, for our answer. Our only safety is in the careful study, in dependence on the Holy Spirit, of what Pentecost and the teaching of inspired Scripture set before us. And if God by His very special revelation of His Son from heaven in Paul gave him for an example and a pledge of what He could do for us, we may be sure that his example of devotion, of self-sacrifice, of joy and of victory, will help us to find the path in which we can live well-pleasing to God.

I know not how I can plead with sufficient earnestness to urge God's children to make their private devotions a means for the cultivation of a clearer insight into what God IS ABSOLUTELY WILLING TO DO FOR US. There is a life awaiting us, prepared by God Himself, and waiting to be revealed in us by the Holy Spirit, if we are only ready to know and confess how very much there is lacking in our spiritual life. Let us but take two simple truths in regard to the Holy Spirit as our guide. The one, that the Church of today is characterised by the feeble workings of the Holy Spirit. The other, that in God's Word there is promised to us the mighty working of God's Spirit in the heart of His children. If we accept the first of these truths, we take our place on the one side, in the penitent confession of how little we have honoured the Holy Spirit, and how little lived up to what He is willing to work in us, we shall find our hearts drawn out to a new and a larger faith in the mighty workings of the Spirit which God has promised. Our devotions each day may become a step out of the human standard we have been content with, and an ever-increasing entrance into a life in the Spirit, which God has so surely provided, and will so certainly make true to us.

As we pursue our study, let us fix our attention on three simple questions. 1. Does Scripture really lay down a standard of attainment for those who wholly yield themselves to the blessed Spirit and trust in God's almighty power Himself to work in them what He asks? 2. Is it true that the Church as a whole does not live up to the standard that God has actually made possible, and is within our reach? 3. Are we ready to yield ourselves with our whole heart to accept what God has prepared?

III

THE GREAT NEED OF THE CHURCH

"Because ye are sons, God sent forth the Spirit of His Son into your hearts, crying 'Abba, Father'."—GAL. iv. 6.

WHEN God had revealed His love in the gift of His Son, His great work was completed. When Christ had died upon the cross, with His "It is finished", and had been raised up again, and seated upon the throne of God, His work was completed. Then began the dispensation of the Spirit, Whose office it was to reveal and impart all that the work of God and of Christ had prepared. This work of the Holy Spirit has not yet been accomplished; it is for this that Christ sits upon the throne, henceforth expecting till all His enemies be made His footstool.

The great difference between the work of the Father and the Son, and the work of the Holy Spirit, is that while the former wrought out their work for and on behalf of men, as a salvation prepared for their acceptance, the office of the Holy Spirit is to impart to them that grace which enables them to accept and to live out what the Father and the Son have provided. The great mark of the operation of the Spirit is, that in this dispensation His work and man's work are inextricably linked together, so that whatever the Spirit does He does through man, and whatever is to be done in the Kingdom of God it is man who does it. In the world of men the Holy Spirit can manifest Himself in no other way than in, and as, the spirit of man. It is the dispensation in which we are to prove what man's part is in the carrying out of God's plan.

When Paul had spoken of God in Christ reconciling the world unto Himself, he immediately adds, "He hath committed unto us the Word of reconciliation." The carrying out and making known of the reconciliation was entrusted to the Church. On its faithfulness or its failure the spread and the power with which that reconciliation would work in the world was to depend.

These thoughts suggest to us the wonderful glory of the ministration of the Spirit, the terrible failure on the part of the Church, and the only path to restoration.

God's great object in sending the Spirit of Christ to take possession of the hearts of men, was to restore the fellowship with Himself for which man had been created. All the work of God and of Christ in redemption culminated in this one thing—the Holy Spirit was to communicate the salvation that had been provided, and to maintain it in unbroken efficacy, moment by moment, in the heart of God's children. He was to be the Spirit of life, leading them in the path of holiness and perfect conformity to Jesus Christ. He was to be the Spirit of power, fitting them for service, as Christ's witnesses, to the ends of the earth. The Holy Spirit was to be the perfect bond of union between the Father in heaven and the child on earth. The bond of union, too, beween Christ and the perishing world. Every believer would, in the power of the Spirit, be able to give his testimony to the love that had come to him. God's great purpose was that man should be saved by man, not only in Christ His Son, but in the men in whom He lived. The gift of the Spirit rendered this possible and certain in everyone who yielded himself absolutely to be possessed by Him.

How terribly the Church has failed in its high calling. How few there have been who with Paul, and those like-

minded, have proved that absolute dependence upon
the Spirit does secure the continual presence and working of God in the life. Is not the great mark of much the
larger part of the Church, the very feeble workings of
the Spirit of God? And is not the reason that there is
so much prayer for the power of the Holy Spirit, with
but little of an answer, because so few are ready to
yield themselves absolutely to His control? They do
not even know that this is the one secret of coming
under His full power—the faith that in unceasing dependence upon His operation dies to self and counts
upon Him to do His perfect work. It is when the
Church, when the believer, begins to understand this,
that there will be a hope for the true revival of the
Spirit in divine power.

Thank God for the assurance that the Spirit has been
given, that He is yearning over us, that He is ready and
able to take possession of His Church. Let us but be
ready to confess honestly the state in which the Church
is, and the share we have in it. Let all who believe in
God, in His love and His almighty power, bear their
testimony to what is the one thing needful, and the one
thing above everything most certain, THAT GOD IS
LONGING TO ENTER IN THE POWER OF THE SPIRIT INTO
POSSESSION OF HIS REDEEMED PEOPLE. And let us lift
the voice heavenward, to plead in unceasing intercession
that God would manifest Himself to all who are longing
to be temples of the Holy Ghost filled with His power,
yielded up to be made meet for the dwelling, the
worship, the service, of the living God.

And what now is the connection between what we
have said and the devotion of daily life? Nothing less
than this, that our aim in our secret devotions must
ever be to cast aside the ordinary standard of religion
and to make God's standard the object of our unceasing
desire. God's Spirit has been given us to reveal Christ

and His life in us. No true progress can be made until
with purpose of heart we consent that in everything
we shall live in immediate and unceasing dependence
on the power of the Spirit.

I have already suggested what will be some of the
great hindrances. No due sense of His claim to have
absolute and entire control. A lack of faith in His
gracious and tender love to meet us and work His work
of power in our hearts. Ignorance of what is meant
by the power of the world as the great enemy of the
blessed Spirit. Unwillingness to take up the cross of
Christ, to die with Him in His death as the Spirit alone
can reveal it. Or to sum up all in one, the absence of that
deep conviction of what a holy, divine, and almighty
work it is for God the Spirit to take possession of our
life and carry out His one desire to make Christ live
within us.

God help us to remember that it is in our daily
devotions that this great work is to be carried on and
accomplished. God help us to be strong in faith, giving
glory to God, trusting in Him Who quickeneth the
dead, and calleth the things that are not as though they
were, to carry out His own work in us. We never can
sufficiently insist upon the thought that the one great
object of God in the gift of the Holy Spirit, was to fit
His people for being and doing what they could not be
and do in the Old Testament. God does not expect
from us, however earnest our efforts and our prayers
may be, that we should strengthen and maintain our
spiritual life. That is the work for which His Holy
Spirit was promised. It is only the soul who lives in
entire surrender to and dependence on the blessed Spirit,
in whom God can effectually carry on His mighty work
and accomplish all His blessed purposes.

IV

THE SPIRITUAL LIFE

"Blessed be the God and Father of our Lord Jesus Christ, Who hath blessed us with every spiritual blessing in the heavenly places in Christ."—EPH. i. 3.

WE propose studying the Epistle to the Ephesians, with a view to the discovery of the New Testament standard of devotion as presented to us by the Apostle Paul. These opening words of the Epistle not only give us a blessed summary of the truth of the Gospel, but reveal, out of the depths of Paul's experience, what the true Christian life is.

The benediction here corresponds to the Apostolical benediction. We have first THE GRACE OF OUR LORD JESUS CHRIST. "The God and Father of our Lord Jesus Christ has blessed us with all spiritual blessings IN HIM." The expression IN HIM is the keynote of the Epistle, occurring more than twenty times. The words of our text are the beginning of a sentence running without stop from verse 3 to 14, in which we find: "chosen in Him," "fore-ordained through Him," "accepted in Him," "redemption in Him," "the purpose of God in Him," "summing up all things in Him", "made an heritage in Him," "in Whom we believed," "in Whom we were sealed with the Holy Spirit." All our blessings are treasured up in Christ; and we ourselves are in Him too. As truly as the blessings are in Christ, so truly is our life in Him; the two are inseparably intertwined; abiding in Christ means an abiding in the heavenly places and in all the spiritual blessings with which God hath blessed us in Him. And faith in Christ is meant to be nothing less than the unceasing dependence and fellowship with Him, and the reception from Him of every grace the soul can possibly need. As absolute and continuous as is the contact with the air which my life needs CAN MY SOUL BE KEPT IN THE BLESSED FELLOWSHIP WITH MY LORD JESUS. This is what Scripture means by the words: "Christ is our Life," "Christ liveth in me," "To me to live is Christ." What riches of grace!

Then comes next THE LOVE OF GOD. It is the Father who hath blessed us in the Son. Christ was the Father's gift to us, and all blessings are given by Him in the same intensity and reality of possession. God's purpose was to bring us back to Himself as our Creator, in Whose fellowship and glory our happiness could alone be found. And God could attain His object, and satisfy the love of His own heart, in no other way but by bringing us into the most complete union with Christ Himself, so that in Him we can be as near to God as Christ is. Oh, the mystery of the love of God!

And of all the blessings that we have in Christ, our text says, "God HATH BLESSED us with all spiritual blessings." More than one believer, as he longed and prayed earnestly for some new revelation of God's grace, has found in these words the very key that he needed to unlock the treasury of blessing. As the light of the Spirit shone upon these words, they became quick with a new meaning. In Christ GOD HATH BLESSED ME with all spiritual blessings. It needs but the rest of faith to accept and the whole-hearted surrender to claim them in Him: the heart finds itself in the very centre of blessing.

Such a sight of what is meant, and such a faith in claiming it, cannot but lead to the adoring benediction: Blessed be the God and Father of our Lord Jesus Christ. As it is the fountain from which, all the Epistle through, the stream of blessings flows, so it may be in our life too an unceasing song of praise: "I will bless the Lord at all times; His praise shall continually be in my mouth."

And now comes THE FELLOWSHIP OF THE SPIRIT. The spiritual blessings are nothing less than Holy-Spirit-blessings. As God, proceeding from the Father and the Son, He has the divine office of conveying and imparting to us all the fulness of blessing and blessedness in the divine life. He reveals them to us. He enables us to see and delight in and accept them. He communicates them so truly in our inmost being that we become spiritual men, endued, clothed with the power of the Spirit. Where the heart is fully yielded to Him, He not only exercises a certain influence, but dwells within us, in a divine reality and power, making our heart the temple of Christ and of God. He imparts to us, as a seed within us, every grace and virtue that there is in Christ, to become our own. What He shows He also works. Just as the seed sown in the earth needs the warmth of the sun and the rain from heaven to make it grow, even so, as we believe that the seeds are within us, we look up to Christ in Whom our life is, and in the sunshine of His love, the spiritual blessings grow up and are wrought into our very being. In every blessing we have the whole of the blessed Trinity: the Father, the Son, and the Holy Spirit.

In the Epistle we have the Holy Spirit mentioned twelve times in different aspects of the wonderful work He does in the believer. As we proceed to study these, the humble inquirer will find a wonderful revelation of what God really meant the life of His child to be,

and how wonderfully He has provided that we should
indeed attain to it. If we are truly desirous to find out
what the New Testament standard of true spiritual
religion is, and what the devotion in our life which
God has made possible for us, and has made abundant
provision for, we shall feel the courage needed for
setting aside every human standard and making God's
purpose our only aim.

Let us begin by taking the benediction with which
the Epistle opens, and in which it reveals to us the
true life of spiritual blessing, and try and make it our
own. Let us, in quiet meditation, wait on the Holy
Spirit to work in our inmost consciousness the faith
—as one whom the Father has blessed in Christ
with every spiritual blessing, I humbly take my place
before Him and say, Blessed be God, Blessed be
God!

One hears many complaints of the lack of spiritual
life, and hears many prayers for its deepening, while
yet there is much ignorance as to what is really needed
to bring a Christian from a feeble to a strong and joyous
life in Christ Jesus. Let us learn the lesson from our
text, that nothing less can meet our need than the
adoring worship of the ever-blessed Trinity. It is upon
God, Who has blessed us in Christ Jesus, on Whom
our expectation is to rest. It is in Christ that God
and His blessings are to be found, if we continue in
close and unceasing fellowship with Him. It is through
the Spirit that the presence of the Father and the Son
in Divine power can be known. The Holy Spirit has
been given to make Christ real to us, and to take every
spiritual blessing and make it ours. A life entirely given
up to the Holy Spirit to be entirely spiritual, a heart
full of faith and confidence that God and Christ and the
Holy Spirit will do their wondrous work within us, a
body yielded to God as a holy, living sacrifice on the

altar for His service, will surely be accepted. God will teach us to sing the song of praise, "Blessed be the God and Father of our Lord Jesus Christ, Who has blessed us with every spiritual blessing in the heavenly places in Christ!"

THE HOLY SPIRIT IN EPHESIANS

V

THE SEALING OF THE SPIRIT

"In Whom having also believed, ye were sealed with the Holy Spirit of promise."—EPH. i. 13.

THE wonderful sentence that began with the spiritual blessing with which God has blessed us in Christ, and through ten verses showed us what we have in Him, closes with that in which all is contained, THE BLESSED SEALING OF THE HOLY SPIRIT. When a king appoints an ambassador or a governor, his commission is sealed with the king's seal, bearing the king's likeness. The Holy Spirit is the seal of our redemption, not in the sense of giving us the assurance of our sonship as something apart from Himself: HE HIMSELF by His life in us is the seal of our sonship. His work is to reveal and glorify Christ in us, the image of the Father, and by fixing our heart and our faith on Him, to transform us into His likeness. What a wonderful thought. None less than the Spirit of the Father and the Son, the bond of union between them, comes to us as the bond of our union with them, giving us the witness of the Divine life within us, and enabling us to live out that life here in the body. IN THE CHRISTIAN LIFE EVERYTHING DEPENDS ON KNOWING THE HOLY SPIRIT AND HIS BLESSED WORK ARIGHT.

First of all, we need to know that He comes to take the mastery of our whole being,—spirit, soul, and body,—and through it all to reveal the life and the power of God as it works in our renewed nature. Just as Christ could not be glorified and receive the Spirit from the Father for us until He had died upon the cross, and parted with that life in which He had borne our sin and the weakness of our nature, so the coming of the Holy Spirit into our hearts in power implies that we yield ourselves to the fellowship of the cross, and consent TO DIE ENTIRELY TO THAT LIFE OF NATURE IN WHICH SELF AND SIN HAVE THEIR POWER, that through the Spirit, the new, the heavenly, life may take complete possession of us.

This entire mastery implies on our side complete surrender and obedience. Peter speaks of the "Holy Ghost, Whom God hath given to them that obey Him". Even as Christ came to do God's will alone, and humbled Himself to the perfect obedience of the Cross, that He might receive the Spirit from the Father and we through Him, so the full experience of the Spirit's power rests entirely on our readiness in everything to deny self, in everything to yield ourselves to His teaching and leading. The great reason that believers are so feeble, and so ignorant of the blessings of the Spirit, is this, that at conversion and in their Christian life the question was never faced and settled that by the grace of God they would in everything, in every place, and at every moment, yield themselves to the control of the Spirit. Oh, that God's children might accept of God's terms, THE UNDIVIDED MASTERY OF THE SPIRIT, the unhesitating surrender of the whole being to His control.

In this connection we need specially to understand that the degree or measure in which the working of the Spirit is experienced may vary greatly. A believer may rejoice in one of the gifts of the Spirit, say peace or joy, zeal or boldness, and yet may be extremely deficient in the other graces which His presence bestows. Our true position towards the blessed Spirit must be that of perfect teachableness, waiting to be led by Him in all the will of God, with the consciousness of how much there still is within the heart that needs to be renewed and sanctified, if He is to have the place and the honour that belong to Him.

There are specially two great enemies under which man was brought by his fall. These are the world and self. Of the world Christ says, "The Spirit of truth, whom the world cannot receive because it knoweth Him not." WORLDLINESS IS THE GREAT HINDRANCE THAT KEEPS BELIEVERS FROM LIVING THE SPIRITUAL LIFE. Of self Christ said, "Let a man deny himself," "Let a man hate his own life." SELF, IN ALL ITS FORMS— SELF-WILL, SELF-PLEASING, SELF-CONFIDENCE—RENDERS A LIFE IN THE POWER OF THE SPIRIT IMPOSSIBLE. And from these two great enemies, the power of the world and the power of self, nothing can deliver us but the Cross of Christ. Paul boasts in the Cross by which he has been crucified to the world. And he tells us: "They that are Christ's have crucified the flesh," in which self has its seat and power. To live the spiritual life nothing less is needed than the entire giving up of the old life to the death, to make room for the blessed Spirit to renew and transform our whole being into the will of God.

Without the Spirit we can do nothing acceptable to God in things great or little. "No man can say that Jesus is Lord but by the Holy Ghost." No man can truly say "Abba, Father," but by the Spirit of God's Son sent into our hearts. In our fellowship with God, and as much in our fellowship with men, in our religious worship and our daily avocations, in the highest pursuit that life can offer and as much in the daily care of our bodies, everything must bear the seal of the Holy Spirit.

Of the Son we read, "Him hath God the Father sealed." It is "in Christ" that we are sealed. As He, when the Spirit had descended upon Him at His baptism, was led by the Spirit to the wilderness, thence by the Spirit to the synagogue in Nazareth, and thence through His whole life to the Cross, "where by the Eternal Spirit He offered Himself a sacrifice unto God, so we too are to live our daily life as those who are sealed by the Spirit. As true as it is of Christ, "Him hath God the Father sealed," is it true of every believer—the Son, and every son, sealed by the Father. The great mark of the New Testament standard of the Christian life and its devotion is to be, that it is all to bear the stamp of the HOLY SPIRIT.

Let us learn the precious lesson that the Holy Spirit cannot inspire our devotions, except as He inspires our daily life. The Spirit of Christ claims and needs the rule of the whole man if He is to perform His blessed work in us. The indwelling of the Holy Spirit means nothing less than that in our religious life—and that means our whole life, nothing excluded—nothing is to be thought of, or trusted to, or sought after, but the immediate and continual dependence on His blessed working. The devotion of our public life will be the test of the uprightness of our secret devotion, and at the same time the means of strengthening our confidence in God Who works in us through His blessed Spirit. Every thought of faith in the power of the Spirit must find its expression in prayer to God, Who will most surely give us His Spirit when we ask Him and work in us through the Spirit what we need.

A seal, attached to a document, gives validity to every sentence and every word it contains. Even so the Holy Spirit of promise, with which we are sealed, ratifies every promise that there is in Christ. And this is now one of the great differences between the Bible and the human standard of the Christian life, that while in the former the seal of the Spirit is accepted in His control of every movement and every moment of our life, in the latter we are content with but a very partial surrender to His guidance.

VI

THE SPIRIT OF WISDOM

"I cease not making mention of you in my prayers, that the Father of glory may give unto you a Spirit of Wisdom and Revelation in the knowledge of Him having the eyes of your heart enlightened, that ye may know."—EPH. i. 16, 17.

No sooner had Paul mentioned the Holy Spirit, as God's seal on believers, than he speaks of his unceasing prayer that God would specially give them the Spirit of Wisdom. It is not enough that the believer has the Holy Spirit; that Spirit can only do His blessed work AS GOD WORKS THROUGH HIM, in answer to prayer. Paul prays unceasingly, and with that teaches them to pray unceasingly too, for the Wisdom of the Spirit to enlighten the eyes of their heart. Just as a child needs education, the believer who has the Spirit within him needs a Divine illumination FROM DAY TO DAY, to know God and the spiritual life He bestows. This life is so supernatural and such a Divine mystery, that without spiritual wisdom and understanding we cannot apprehend it. (Note 1, p. 128.)

We need to know three things. First, what "the hope of His calling" is; the high and holy and heavenly calling of which we are to walk worthily. Then, "the riches of the glory of God's inheritance in the saints"; what the unsearchable riches are of the heavenly treasure which God has in His saints. And lastly, and very specially, "the power" by which we can fulfil

our calling and possess our heritage, "THE EXCEEDING
GREATNESS OF HIS POWER TO USWARD WHO BELIEVE."
The life the Christian has to live here on earth is so
truly the life of God in the soul, that nothing that we
can do can maintain that life, or renew it. It is a life
that we have in Christ; it is a life to be received out of
Christ by faith daily and hourly. It is a life which the
omnipotence of God Himself alone can begin and carry
on. And the great need of the believer is to wait upon
God for the Holy Spirit to show "the exceeding greatness of His power to usward who believe". No human
mind can grasp it; the Holy Spirit living in the heart
reveals it, and teaches us to believe it, and to expect it.
As Christians we need to know that we are to depend
every day upon God to work in us according to "the
exceeding greatness of His strength in us who believe,"
and every day to accept the Holy Spirit's teaching in
answer to prayer, to keep us conscious of this mighty
power working in us. (Note 2, p. 128.)

With regard to this mighty power dwelling in us the
Holy Spirit shows us what its work and nature is. It
is the power of God, "according to that working of the
strength of His might which He wrought in Christ
when He raised Him from the dead, and made Him to
sit at His right hand." It is this power that works in
us who believe, to raise us up from a life under the
power of death to a life in the glory of heaven. It is
by the exceeding greatness of this power to usward
who believe that our daily life has to be lived, in fellowship with the life of the Son of God. God raised Christ
from the dead because His death on the cross had been
the exhibition of the deepest humility and the most
perfect obedience. Because He had yielded Himself
unreservedly to the power of God, both in His life and
suffering, and in His surrender to death and the grave,
God raised Him from the dead and gave Him glory.

And even so when we give ourselves over to die with Christ to sin and the world and the flesh, in a Christ-like humility and obedience, the exceeeding greatness of His power will work in us to make us partakers, day by day, of the resurrection power, and of the Spirit of glory which followed it.

This thought of the life of the believer as being the exhibition of "the exceeding greatness of God's power in us who believe," runs through all the writings of Paul. In his prayer for the Colossians (i. 10), he asks that they may "walk worthily of the Lord unto all pleasing, bearing fruit unto every work, and increasing in the knowledge of God." And then he adds, "STRENGTHENED WITH ALL POWER, ACCORDING TO THE MIGHT OF HIS GLORY, unto all patience and long-suffering with joy." As one thinks of the life of devotion which Paul here holds up, always worthy of God and pleasing to Him, always fruitful in every good work, always increasing in the living knowledge of God, and always persevering with all patience and long-suffering, one feels that the standard is an impossible one. But then the thought comes in, "STRENGTHENED WITH ALL POWER, ACCORDING TO THE MIGHT OF HIS GLORY," and we say—No, if this be true, if God works this, the life is possible. In our own Epistle the same thought occurs (iii. 20), "Now unto Him that is able to do above all that we ask or think, ACCORDING TO THE POWER THAT WORKETH IN US, unto Him be the glory for ever and ever"; the words lift our heart to believe and expect something far beyond what we ask or think. The life we are to live is to be a supernatural one; it is to be the resurrection life; yea, more, THE HEAVENLY LIFE OF CHRIST IN GLORY MAINTAINED IN US BY THE SAME WORKING OF THE STRENGTH OF HIS MIGHT by which He raised Christ from the Cross to the Throne. The very same Almighty Power by which Christ was

raised from the dead as the conqueror of sin and death,
is the power that works in our hearts to give us too the
victory over every sin. To believe this with our whole
heart will at once bring us to a sense of our utter impotence, but also of the Divine certainty that God will
fulfil His purpose in us.

If the believer will but trust the exceeding greatness
of His power; will but yield himself in entire subjection
to let that power rule in his heart, and do all its will
there; if he will be content, amid perfect ignorance
and impotence, to trust the strength that is made perfect
in weakness; if he will but count all things loss for the
sake of this blessed prize;—God's Word is pledged that
the power that raised Christ shall work in him day by
day until he shall know what it is here to live and reign
with Christ in glory.

We are trying to discover what the New Testament
standard of a life of true devotion is, and whether the
accepted standard of our modern Christianity is in
harmony with it. Do let us try to sum up in our own
mind what the full meaning is of Paul's prayer. Think of
his private devotions pleading for his Ephesians. Think
of what the standard of his own life must have been, as
he speaks so often of God's working in him (Col. i. 29;
1 Cor. v. 10; 2 Cor. iii. 5, iv. 7, xii. 9, 10; Phil.
iv. 13). Think of what he wished his readers to take
as their aim and expectation. Think of how his whole
soul was set upon the two great thoughts: every believer to live every day under the teaching of the Holy
Spirit, and under the mighty power of God working
in him. And then pause and ask whether your secret
devotion, and your confident faith, and your hope in
daily life, have consented to accept and rejoice in the
life that is held out to us here—daily to live out
the exceeding greatness of God's power working
in you, and daily to yield yourself to the Holy Spirit

to keep dependent on that power. (Note 3, p. 129.)

May God help us to return and return again to this passage, till it becomes to us through the Holy Spirit the very light of God shining in our heart, and the power of God working in our life!

VII

THE SPIRIT OF ACCESS

"Through Him we both have our access in one Spirit unto the Father."—EPH. ii. 18 (comp. iii. 12).

HAVE you ever noticed the wonderful beauty of the passage that leads up to the words of our text? In vers. 4–10 we have the setting forth of the great salvation with which God has visited us, in connection with the words, "By grace have ye been saved through faith". With regard to each of these words you have a sacred quartette.

"YE ARE SAVED": "God hath quickened us together with Christ,"—"And raised us up with Him,"—"And made us to sit with Him in the heavenly places,"—"We are His workmanship, created in Christ Jesus for good works." What a salvation, all the work of God in us!

"BY GRACE": that points to what had been said—"God Who is rich in mercy,"—"For His great love wherewith He loved us,—That in the ages to come" (that is from the resurrection onward) "He might show the exceeding riches of His grace"—"In kindness towards us in Christ Jesus." What a riches and a glory of God's grace!

"THROUGH FAITH." "Not of yourselves,"—"It is the gift of God,"—"Not of works,"—"Created for good works, which God afore prepared." What a salvation and what a grace prepared for faith to receive and live in!

Then follows (vers. 11–17) the way in which these Gentiles had been led to the knowledge of that salvation. "Made nigh in the blood of Christ," with Christ their peace destroying the enmity, and reconciling Jew and Gentile in one body unto God through the cross. And so we reach our text: "For through Him we both have access in one Spirit unto the Father." Here again we have the blessed Trinity, with the precious lesson that the great work in which Christ and the Holy Spirit are united is to make the permanent and unceasing presence of God a blessed reality. Our text not only speaks of a right of access, but of its actual enjoyment, as secured to us through Christ and His Spirit.

ACCESS TO THE FATHER. Think of what Scripture teaches us. In the tabernacle, the Holiest of all, in which God dwelt, was separated by a thick veil from the Holy Place in which the priests came daily to serve. Not even the High Priest might enter that Holiest of all, except on one day of the year. Access through the veil was forbidden on pain of death. When Christ died, this veil was rent. Christ Jesus not only entered into God's Presence with His blood, but He opened a new and living way through the rent veil of His flesh for us to enter too. When the veil was rent in the tabernacle the way was opened, not only to the High Priest, but to all the priests. When Jesus entered heaven the way was opened for every believer to enter into God's holy Presence, not for a time, but to dwell there every day and all the day. Jesus sent down out of heaven the Holy Spirit, Whom, as Son of Man, He had received from the Father, to bring us into that holy Presence, and enable us to live in it. The unbroken enjoyment of God's presence is possible to every believer who will forsake all to possess it.

THROUGH THE SON: that does not only mean as our Advocate, who secures our acquittance and acceptance.

It means much more. Our High Priest lives and acts in the power of an endless, incorruptible life. All He works in us is in the power of His resurrection life, and His entrance into glory. To have access to God through Christ means that, as those "who have been quickened together with Christ and made to sit with Him in the heavenly places," we live in Him, we are one with Him, we abide in Him, and are by Him ever brought and kept in the fellowship with God. The access through Christ brings us as near to God as Christ is, in an intimate, Divine fellowship that passes all understanding.

In one Spirit. The Spirit has been given us that we may have the power to cry "Abba, Father," even as Christ did. The Spirit dwells in us to reveal Christ; without Him no man can in truth call Jesus Lord. The Spirit takes possession of our whole life and being; where He is yielded to and trusted, He maintains the fellowship with the Father through the Son, in the Holiest of all, a Divine reality in our life experience.

Such is the New Testament standard of Christian living; entrance and access to God's holy presence and love through the living union with Christ in the power of the Holy Spirit. The one thing that is needed to make it ours is—the practice of the presence of God; the giving of our life to the death, that Christ's life, as He sought on earth even to please the Father, may be carried out in us. Nothing less will avail but this— access through Christ, in the Spirit, restoring to us what Adam had lost in the fall, a walk in the light of God, as clear and natural as is the enjoyment of the sun to our bodies. No thinking, no feeling, no working, can enable us to dispense with the actual exercise, day by day, of the privilege of access into the Holiest of all, and of dwelling there.

Most of us are familiar with the hymn, "Take time

to be holy." I was struck by the use of the expression in the *Life of Griffith John*. After being in China more than twenty years, he often said to young missionaries, "Preach the Gospel, AND TAKE TIME TO BE HOLY AS THE PREPARATION." In the Mission Conference in Shanghai, in 1877, he said, "The missionary must above everything BE A HOLY MAN; the Chinese expect it of him. I am persuaded that no minister can be a great spiritual power in whom this is not in good measure seen. He must be more than a good man; a man WHO TAKES TIME, NOT ONLY TO MASTER THE LANGUAGE AND THE LITERATURE OF THE PEOPLE, BUT TO BE HOLY. . . . Brethren, this is what we need if this empire is to be moved by us. To this end the throne of grace must be our refuge; the shadow of the Almighty MUST EVERY DAY AND EVERY HOUR BE OUR DWELLING, we must take time to be filled with His power, we must TAKE TIME TO BE HOLY."

It is he who takes time to avail himself fully of access to the Holiest of all, where God dwells and reveals Himself through Christ in the Spirit, on whom the blessed truth will dawn that full fellowship with God in His holiness will make us holy too. It is this will make the inner chamber the school of true devotion.

Take time with God, the thrice Holy One. Take time with the Father, of Whom it is said: "The God of peace Himself sanctify you wholly. Faithful is He which calleth you, Who also will do it." Take time with Christ, the Holy One of God, Who spake, "Holy Father, for their sakes I sanctify Myself, that they themselves also may be sanctified in truth." Take time with the Holy Spirit, the Spirit of God's holiness, making you His holy temple. Give time to this holy fellowship; God Himself will sanctify you wholly. Live in the unbroken experience. Through Christ we have our access in one Spirit unto the Father.

VIII

THE TEMPLE OF THE SPIRIT

"Christ Jesus Himself being the chief corner stone, in whom all the building, fitly framed together, groweth into a Holy Temple in the Lord; in whom ye also are builded together for a habitation of God in the Spirit."—EPH. ii. 20–22.

WE have here again the blessed Trinity. The Father, God, for Whom the habitation is built. The Son, Jesus Christ, the chief corner stone, in Whom the holy temple groweth. The Spirit, the Builder, through Whom all the living stones are united with each other and with the chief corner stone, and thus in perfect fellowship with God. As in heaven, so in the Church on earth, and in the heart of every believer, the thrice Holy One is the God of our salvation.

The great thought of the passage is fellowship—the fellowship of the Spirit, as seen in the temple. That fellowship is spoken of first as THE FELLOWSHIP OF BELIEVERS, built up into one holy temple. From verse 11 Paul had spoken of the Gentiles as strangers from the covenant of the promise, who are now made nigh in the blood of Christ; of the enmity being abolished and nailed to the Cross, that WE BOTH might have access in one Spirit unto the Father. In verse 19 he says, "ye are no more strangers but fellow citizens, and of the household of God." As Jew and Gentile both had access by one Spirit unto the Father, so here by the same Spirit they are built up into one temple. The cross has

made an end of all separation among men, Jews and
Gentiles, Greek and barbarian, the wise and the foolish,
—all are one in Christ Jesus. National and social
distinctions are as nothing compared to that unity which
the Spirit gives in Christ Jesus. The cement by which
the living stones are held together, the bond by which
all are members of one household and one body, is
nothing less than the Spirit and the Life and the Love
of God Himself.

THE FELLOWSHIP WITH CHRIST THE CORNERSTONE is
also the work of the Blessed Spirit. In Him the believer
on earth and the Father in heaven find their bond of
union. We often suffer much, even in religion, from
regarding as an end what is only a means. Men think of
pardon and of peace, of obedience and of holiness, as
an end, while they are only means to the great end of
bringing God and man into perfect union. When we
speak of the Mosaic worship, how we prize and press
the thought of the atonement through blood, and the
access of the High Priest to sprinkle that blood on the
mercy-seat, as the image of what Christ has done for
us, while we forget there was something higher,—
nothing less than the presence and fellowship of God
Himself. God dwelt in the sanctuary in the midst of
His people that He might be their God, and that they
might enjoy His guidance and His blessing, His mighty
deliverance in their time of need, and His abiding Presence. And this is what we need above everything to
fix our hearts on in God's word, THAT FELLOWSHIP
WITH THE FATHER AND THE SON, THAT COMMUNION,
INTIMATE, HOLY, AND UNCEASING, is what man was
created for, and has been restored to, in Christ Jesus.

As believers accept and realise their dependence on
Christ, their inseparable union with Him, and trust the
blessed Spirit ever to maintain within them the faith
of His Presence, they will come to know that the

Presence and the Power of God is the highest of all the blessings with which He has blessed us in Christ Jesus.

In the Apostolic benediction "the fellowship of the Spirit" indicates what His chief work is. THROUGH HIM ALONE can we have our access in Christ to the Father. He reveals Christ to us and the reality of our union with Him, and the nearness to God which He gives. He not only builds the temple, but reveals the indwelling God. He not only builds the temple as a whole, but makes each heart a temple, and reveals how God is willing and able to be and to do in our heart what He is and does in His heaven above. Yes, what to so many Christians appears an impossibility, THAT THE PRESENCE OF GOD HIMSELF CAN BE WITH THEM AND CAN KEEP THEM ALL THE DAY, is indeed possible, if we know and believe in the Holy Spirit as the power of God that worketh in us.

The fellowship with God, with Christ the chief cornerstone, and with each other, constitutes the blessedness of our being built as an habitation of God in the Spirit. We need to know how in the Cross of Christ all selfishness has been destroyed, and the love that seeks no life but giving itself for others has been made possible to us. We shall then understand that a close fellowship with each other is as sacred and indispensable as the fellowship with God is. We shall not only see how entirely our spiritual life depends upon it, but how there is no way of proving to men our love to God, and the reality of God's love to us, but through the love of the brethren. When our Lord Jesus prayed, in the last night, "that they may be one, even as we are one, that the world may know that Thou lovedst them, even as Thou lovedst Me," He taught us that a divided church is powerless before the enemy; a love to the brethren like God's and Christ's will give us the victory. The world will be compelled to acknowledge that Christ crucified in His love is present and working in us. As one has said, "If without recognising the Unity of the Body, Pentecostal power were again to be made manifest, the Churches would appropriate the glory to themselves, and would not lay it down at the feet of the King."

When the New Testament standard of the spiritual life is lifted up, and the love of the brethren takes the place God's Word has given it as the only proof of the reality of our love to God, and of the conformity of our life to the image of Jesus Christ and His love on the cross, our devotions will be delivered from the selfishness that so often hinders them. Our hearts will feel a new confidence that God will hear the prayers in which the Spirit teaches us to plead for the growing of a holy temple in the Lord, a fit and worthy habitation of God in the Spirit. And we shall learn that by the power of the Holy Spirit God's presence with us, and our devotion to Him, can be the mark of our life all the day.

IX

THE SPIRIT OF MISSIONS

"The mystery of Christ, as it hath now been revealed unto His holy apostles and prophets in the Spirit, that the Gentiles are fellow-heirs, and fellow-members of the body, and fellow-partakers of the promise in Christ Jesus."—EPH. iii. 4–6.

THE more one studies the Epistle to the Ephesians, the deeper becomes the impression that the standard of New Testament religion it sets before us is but faintly realised in the Church. Its whole tone is so intensely supernatural that nothing less is needed than a life identified with the life of Christ, and under the unceasing presence and guidance of the Holy Spirit, to fulfil its meaning.

In the first chapter of our Epistle Paul set before us THE SOURCE OF THE DIVINE LIFE, followed by the unceasing prayer that that life might be revealed by the Holy Spirit in the heart of his readers. In chap. ii we had THE COMMUNICATION OF THAT LIFE, God Himself quickening us in Christ, and making us His workmanship, created in Christ Jesus unto good works. And now in chap. iii we are taught that THE PROCLAMATION OF THAT DIVINE LIFE is equally the work of God and His Spirit. As definitely as the origin and communication of His life is a supernatural one, so the provision for its being made known in the world is entirely supernatural too. We have here the exceeding glory of God's grace set before us in a new light. In chap. i we had "His grace which He freely bestowed on us in the beloved, with the forgiveness of our sins, according to the riches of His grace." In chap. ii we had "the exceeding riches of His grace, which in the ages to come He would show forth in us." And now in chap. iii we have "the dispensation of that grace of God which was given to His holy apostles and prophets in the Spirit," and of which Paul was made a minister, "according to the gift of that grace of God which was given me according to His power." In the ministry of the Gospel the riches of God's grace are to be very specially manifested and magnified. Paul speaks of the "mystery of Christ," and says it has now been revealed by the Holy Spirit, that the Gentiles are fellow-heirs, and fellow-members, and fellow-partakers in Christ Jesus. Of this mystery he has been made a minister. And as it was through the Spirit that the revelation of what had been hid in God through the ages was revealed, so it was under the presence and direction of the Holy Spirit that the work was begun and was to be carried out, of bringing the Gospel to every creature. We read in Acts, "the Spirit said" to Philip, to speak to the man of Ethiopia; "the Spirit said to Peter" to go to Cornelius; "the Holy Ghost said" to the praying company at Antioch, "Separate Me Barnabas and Saul." "It seemed good to the Holy Ghost" that liberty should be given to the Gentiles in Antioch. We read of Paul's "being forbidden of the Holy Ghost" to speak the Word in Asia, and of "the Spirit of Jesus not suffering" them to go into Bithynia. Paul speaks of what Christ wrought through him for the obedience of the Gentiles "in the power of the Holy Ghost," and of his ministering the Gospel, that the offering up of the Gentiles might be acceptable, "being sanctified by the Holy Ghost." And elsewhere he speaks of his preaching among the Gentiles, being "in power and in the Holy Ghost and in much assurance," even as they also "received the Word with joy of the Holy Ghost." To the Holy Ghost was entrusted the whole work of revealing and carrying out through the succeeding ages the riches of the glory of this mystery among the Gentiles—"Christ in you, the hope of glory." All mission work has been placed under the direction of the Holy Spirit; in every department of that work His guidance is to be sought for, and can be counted upon. Missions are indeed the work of the Holy Spirit (Acts i. 8).

We may well ask how it comes that in these days we so little use the language of Scripture in regard to our Mission work. It is to be feared that it is greatly owing to a lack of that living faith in the Holy Spirit, whose it is to reveal the great mystery of God in the heart, to rouse its affections and its purpose, and to empower for all the service that is needed to carry out God's blessed will. It is not enough that to the prophets and the apostles, to preachers and believers of true devotion, the Spirit should reveal this hidden mystery of God, so that through them the Church may become acquainted with His plans. Each one who hears needs individually to receive the teaching of the Spirit, if the blessed secret is really to master and possess him. We count it a great step in advance when a Church or a congregation has yielded itself to the call to take a part in the great work of evangelising the nations. And yet this may possibly be nothing more than from a sense of duty and a readiness to take a part in all the activities of the Church. Much more is needed if believers are indeed to be brought under the influence of the great truth that Missions are the chief aim of the Church, the one object for which every congregation, and therefore every individual believer, exists. It is when the Holy Spirit is honoured and waited on, when in preaching and in writing, in prayer and in Christian intercourse, when in all work within the Church to train her for her great calling, and in all work in the Mission field to conquer the heathen for Christ, THE DEPENDENCE UPON THE HOLY SPIRIT IS COUNTED THE FIRST AND ESSENTIAL ELEMENT OF SUCCESS, that the Church will be able to carry out its Lord's commands. When the Holy Spirit, in our missionary committees and meetings and conferences, takes the place that was given to Him in primitive Church, we may expect that His power will be manifested as in the early days.

"Ye shall receive power when the Holy Ghost is come upon you; and ye shall be My witnesses unto the uttermost parts of the earth." These were the very last words of our Lord upon earth. They linked the promise of the Spirit with the ends of the earth. The fulness of the Spirit will only be given in connection with the extension of the Kingdom. The power for carrying the Gospel to those near or far off is absolutely dependent on the measure of the Spirit's presence. Every prayer for the power of the Spirit to be revealed ought to have as its aim the power to testify for Jesus. As the numbers of believers increase, who have power to prevail with God in prayer for the Spirit, will the Church become strong for preaching the Gospel to every creature.

The connection between these thoughts and our life of secret devotion is close and vital. Paul spoke to believers of "the conflict" he had in unceasing prayer for the Churches among the heathen, even those he had not yet seen. He asked them "to labour and strive with him in prayer" for his work of preaching to the Gentiles. Prayer was not to be only for the supply of the needs of the spiritual life, but a training school for the exercise of the highest powers of our being in God's service, as a conflict with the powers of darkness, as a fellowship with the cross and its intercession, as a stirring up of our strength to take hold of God, and to prevail with Him for His blessing on men around us. It is as in secret prayer the consciousness grows in an increasing number of believers, amid the deep sense of unworthiness and helplessness, "I have power with God; He will listen to me; He will give an answer," that our Mission work will become more than ever a triumph of the Cross in its power on our own life, before the Throne of heaven, and on the battle-field in heathendom.

Let us test our devotions by the bearing they have, and the influence they really exercise, on the fulfilment of the mystery of Christ in the world. Let us believe that in the inner chamber the work can be done that will count for eternity, and that there the power can be received that will make itself felt in whatever sphere God allots us in the establishment of His kingdom upon earth. And let us not fear in our measure to say what Paul said of himself, "Unto me, who am less than the least of all saints, is this grace given, to make known unto the Gentiles the unsearchable riches of Christ."

Let our devotions ever be an entire yielding to the blessed Spirit. We may count upon Him to lead us into the riches of the glory of this mystery among the Gentiles. And our prayer will increasingly become for the power of the Holy Spirit to permeate all that is being done for Mission work, whether within the Church, or through it among the heathen.

X

THE SPIRIT OF POWER

"I bow my knees unto the Father that He would grant you, according to the riches of His glory, that ye may be strengthened with power through His Spirit in the inward man, that Christ may dwell in your hearts through faith."[1]—EPH. iii. 14-17.

HERE we have, in this wonderful prayer, once again the blessed Trinity. The Father granting the Spirit of power; the Spirit revealing Christ in the heart; that through Christ and the Spirit we may be filled unto all the fulness of God! As God dwells in heaven as the Three One, even so in our hearts.

In the prayer at the close of chap. i we had the SPIRIT OF WISDOM, that we might know God in the exceeding greatness of His power to us who believe. Here we have the prayer for the SPIRIT OF POWER to strengthen us with might; the exceeding greatness of God's power is to be the permanent experience in our inner life. Let us bow with deep reverence as we gaze upon this mystery of love.

Note first the expression, "that He would grant you ACCORDING TO THE RICHES OF HIS GLORY." Paul wants us to take time and think of the glory, and of its inconceivable riches, and then in faith to expect that God will do nothing less to us than according to the riches of that glory. What is to be done in our inner man is to be in very deed the glory of God shining into our heart, and manifesting the riches of His power in what

[1] See note, p. 102.

49

He does there within us. Again I say, our faith dare not
expect the fulfilment of the prayer until it enters into
and claims to the full that God will do in us "according
to the riches of His glory". Let us take time and see
that nothing less than this is to be the measure of our
faith.

And what is it now that we are to expect? "That
He would grant you TO BE STRENGTHENED WITH MIGHT
BY HIS SPIRIT IN THE INNER MAN." The Spirit is indeed
the mighty power of God. As the Spirit of Wisdom,
He reveals the exceeding greatness of God's power in us
who believe, nothing less than the power that lifted
Christ from the Cross to the Throne. When He has
taught us to see and desire and believe in this exceeding
greatness of God's power IN US, then, as the Spirit of
Power, He works in us, strengthening us with might
in the inner man. In His Word God continually calls
upon His servants to be strong and of good courage.
God chooses the weak things of this world; but when
once they are truly weak, He wants them to be strong
in faith and strong in the power of His might, with
strength of will, ready to do all God says, and strength
of character, bold for any sacrifice. Just as in a healthy
body the strength is not something separated from the
whole, but fills the entire being, and permeates every
fibre, so to be strengthened with might by the Spirit in
the inner man simply means that our whole nature and
being is under the sway of His mighty quickening
power.

The object of this strengthening with might is three-
fold. First of all: "THAT CHRIST DWELL IN THE HEART
BY FAITH." The Divine power enables and emboldens
our faith to claim this precious privilege of the fulfilment
of the promise in John xiv. In the prayer in chap. i
the Spirit was to reveal to us Christ, through the mighty
power of God seated upon the throne, and all things

subject to Him, as the object of our faith. Here the
Saviour comes nearer; the Spirit reveals Him dwelling
within us, and gives the consciousness of His unceasing
and omnipotent presence. Just as surely as God maintains the life of the body by supporting the heart in its
action, will the Holy Spirit, by His almighty Power,
strengthen our inward man day by day to enable us to
live the true spiritual life. Christ's dwelling in the
heart is meant to be our portion.

Then comes the second promise. Where Jesus
Christ is near, ever within us, we are "ROOTED AND
GROUNDED IN LOVE," and comprehend something of the
reality and the joy of the love of Christ that passeth
knowledge.

And this, again, leads on to "BEING FILLED WITH THE
FULNESS OF GOD." The Spirit of Power filling the inner
man, the presence of Christ filling the heart, the fulness
of God filling all.

No wonder that Paul says, "Now, unto Him that is
able to do exceeding abundantly above what we can
ask or think, according to the power that worketh in us,
to Him be glory for ever and ever." The faith in the
promise of what the Father of glory will do, according
to the riches of His glory, will teach us to worship in
deep prostration, in which we can only say, Glory,
glory to Him for ever and ever.

This doxology is in reality a revelation of what lies
at the root of Paul's standard of prayer and expectation
and attainment. He was filled with the one thought,
that what he had asked in the prayer that believers
might be strengthened with might in the inner man,
according to the riches of God's glory, was an experience that could and would be granted. He knew how
many would be ready to say that it was meant to be an
ideal to stir our desires, but that its actual fulfilment in
life in this world was beyond our reach. He felt how

such a thought cuts away the very root of the faith in the supernatural power of God in our lives as being what is absolutely secured in the promise, and therefore possible in experience. He dares any reader to say that what he had asked for out of the riches of God's glory— the strengthening with Divine power, the continual indwelling of Christ in the heart, such a rooting in love as to know the love of Christ which passes knowledge, and as to be filled with all the fulness of God,—he dares any reader to say that this is too high and beyond what we dare think or ask. He knew so certainly that what the exceeding greatness of God's power had done and was doing in his own life, He was ready to do in any one who would give himself up with his whole heart and life to trust God. He answers every doubt, and encourages every sincere soul who is willing to trust God for the fulfilment of the prayer, to say with him: "Now unto Him,"—let us pause and say with him humbly and reverently,—"Now unto Him, WHO IS ABLE to do exceeding abundantly above all that we can ask or think according to the power that worketh in us, be glory in Christ Jesus, world without end. Amen."

Here is Paul's standard of the New Testament life. Is it ours? Do I believe it?—with my whole heart and soul? Does it animate my private devotion in the closet? Does it inspire my life's devotion, as indeed the best and the happiest thing there is in the world?

Let us return to the opening words: "I BOW MY KNEES TO THE FATHER," and plead for ourselves, for all in our charge, for all God's people, THE STRENGTHEN-ING WITH MIGHT ACCORDING TO THE RICHES OF HIS GLORY. God waits to do it. Who will wait to receive it?

And what is more, who will yield himself, like Paul, to be an intercessor, pleading not only with, but also for, the believers around him, that they may so learn to expect the almighty power of God to work in them, that what has hitherto appeared beyond their reach, may become the object of their longing desire and their confident assurance—a life of faith in which Christ in the heart shall live in them?

XI

THE UNITY OF THE SPIRIT

"I beseech you to walk worthily of the calling wherewith ye were called, with all lowliness and meekness, forbearing one another in love, giving diligence to keep the unity of the Spirit in the bond of peace."—EPH. iv. 1–3.

ALL Bible students know that the Epistle to the Ephesians is divided into two equal halves. In chapters i to iii we have the Divine life in its heavenly origin as revealed in the heart of man by the Holy Spirit. In chapters iv to vi we have the Christian life in the ordinary intercourse and conduct of our daily walk. The two halves correspond to what we said of devotion as an act, and as a habit. The first three chapters begin with an act of adoration: "Blessed be God, who hath blessed us," and tell of what all those blessings are. They end with the ascription of glory to Him who is able to do above all that we can ask or think. In every act of prayer and praise, the soul takes its place in the midst of all those riches and seeks to enter more fully into their possession. The last three chapters begin with: "Walk worthy of your high calling," and teach us how to prove our devotion as a habit of the soul in all the most common actions of daily life. As in the Epistle, so in our experience, devotion lifts us up into the Heavenlies to return to this earth so charged with its blessings that, in all our tempers and actions, we may prove that, even as our prayers, so our whole life is devoted to God alone.

The opening words of the second half bring us down at once to the very roots of the Christian life: "Walk worthy of your high calling, with ALL LOWLINESS AND MEEKNESS, giving diligence to keep the unity of the Spirit in the bond of peace." The great mark of the HIGH calling is a Christ-like humility. In the following verse we shall have "one Body and Spirit," and the further setting forth of what the Spirit does as THE SPIRIT OF UNITY. But in our text we have the UNITY OF THE SPIRIT as it is to be maintained in the daily intercourse with our fellow-believers. Amid all diversity of character, and all the temptations arising from the imperfections and evil of those around us, the first mark of true devotion, a life wholly devoted and given up to God, is this, "Walk with ALL LOWLINESS AND MEEKNESS."

To realise the full import of the injunction first look at it in its connection with the three first chapters. Think of the heavenly blessings with which God has blessed us as they are there set forth. Think of the exceeding greatness of His power to usward who believe. Think of the Holy Spirit, by Whom that power is to be revealed in us; through Whom we have access to God in Christ, and are built up as an habitation of God; through Whom we are to be mightily strengthened according to the riches of God's glory, so that Christ can dwell in our hearts. Think of the doxology: "Now unto Him that is able to do exceeding abundantly above all that we can ask or think, according to the power that worketh in us,"—to make all these promises true in us,—"to Him be glory for ever and ever." Take time and form some real true conception of the wonderful standard of spiritual life indicated in these words. And then note the transition: "Walk worthy of this high calling in ALL LOWLINESS AND MEEKNESS." The one fruit of this astonishing revelation of the grace of God, the one mark that you are truly a partaker of it, will be A DEEP AND NEVER CEASING humility, as the proof that God has come to you and revealed Himself, and brought everything like self and its pride down into the very dust.

And if you would enter still more deeply into the meaning of the words, just think that this lowliness and meekness do not comprise your disposition and attitude only towards God, but specially towards man. "In all LOWLINESS AND MEEKNESS, with long-suffering, forbearing one another in love." You can have no surer proof that God's spiritual blessings in Christ Jesus have reached and mastered a man than his LOWLINESS AND MEEKNESS in his intercourse with his fellowmen. The exceeding greatness of God's power in us who believe, raising us out of the death, to self and sin with Christ Jesus to the throne, "seated with Him in the heavenly places," makes us like Christ, willing to wear the servant's garb and do the servant's work. What is impossible with men is possible with God.

How surely this is the true Christlike disposition we see from Paul's words to the Philippians: "Do nothing through vain glory but in LOWLINESS OF MIND, each counting the other better than himself." As the Master Himself, the meek and lowly Lamb of God, had spoken, "Learn of Me, for I am meek and lowly of heart," so Paul enforces what he has written, by adding, "Have this mind in you which was also in Christ Jesus," Who emptied Himself, taking the form of a servant, becoming obedient even unto death, yea, the death of the cross. The self-emptying in the heavenly glory, the form of a servant during all His earthly life, and then the humbling of Himself to the death of the cross,—such was the mind of Christ. It is in this our salvation is rooted; it is in the participation in this that salvation consists; it is in the spirit and practice of a life like this—with all lowliness and meekness, with long-suffering, forbearing one another in love—that Christ will be magnified and our hearts sanctified, and the true witness be given that we have been with Jesus.

And it is thus alone that we give diligence to keep the "Unity of the Spirit in the bond of peace." It is not what we know, or think, or speak of the beauty of love, and the unity of the body, and the power of the Holy Spirit, that proves the true Christian life. It is in the meekness and lowliness of Christ, in daily intercourse with our fellow-Christians, even when they tempt and try us, that we are to show that we will sacrifice anything to maintain the unity of the Spirit, and the bond of love unbroken. It is he that is servant of all to whom Jesus gives the name of chief. It may not be easy; but Christ came from heaven to bring humility back to this earth, and to work it out in our hearts.

Let us ask whether, in the teaching and preaching of the Church, this LOWLINESS AND MEEKNESS OF CHRIST has the place it holds in the Will and the Word of God. Whether in the fellowship of Christians, as far as we know them, there is the endeavour to maintain this standard of Christian living, and to keep the unity of the Spirit from being disturbed by ought of pride or of self. And whether in our own life, and our search after the deepening of the spiritual life, this meekness and lowliness, so pleasing to God, so glorious as seen in Christ Jesus, so beautiful as a grace in a believer, is in very deed our heart's desire and our confident hope. Oh, let it be in every act of devotion the first thing we ask of God, a heart humbled and brought low by His infinite love, and yielded to His Holy Spirit to work out in us, and in His Body around us, the blessed likeness of Jesus our Lord. By the Spirit's aid it can become the undertone and the habit of a life devoted to God.

We are studying the work of the Holy Spirit. Let us not forget to link the thought of a Christ-like lowliness with Him and His power. It was in the power of the Spirit that Christ was led to humble Himself upon the cross as a sacrifice to God. It is only as we claim and receive, and fully yield ourselves to the life of the Spirit, that the meekness and lowliness of our Lord can be found in us. Let us believe mightily that He can and will indeed work it in us.

XII

THE SPIRIT OF UNITY

"There is one body and one Spirit."—EPH. iv. 4.

IN our last chapter our subject was the UNITY OF THE SPIRIT as it is to be maintained in intercourse with fellow-Christians in all lowliness and meekness, with long-suffering, forbearing one another in love. Here our subject is the SPIRIT OF UNITY, as He is the source and the power in which believers, as members of one body in Christ Jesus, are to minister to each other for the building up of the Body of Christ. The knowledge of what the Body of Christ means, the insight into its glory and its purpose, and the fulfilling of the place and ministry to which God has called us in the Body, have a deeper connection with the spiritual life than is generally thought. To receive the Spirit and the love of Christ into the heart in truth means death to every vestige of selfishness, means the surrender as a member of the body, so to give our life and love entirely to Christ and His Body that the welfare of every member within our reach shall become the supreme object of our desire. Let us try to realise what this Body is in which the blessed Spirit of God seeks to manifest Himself.

We know what a masterpiece of the Divine workmanship a human body is, made of the dust, and yet the fit habitation and instrument in which the invisible life can unfold and express itself. But this is but an image and a parable of that Body of which Christ is the Head.

In regard to it our Epistle tells us (i. 22, 23) that God "gave Christ to be the Head over all things to the Church, which is HIS BODY, the fulness of Him that filleth all in all," the Body which is to contain and to exhibit the Divine fulness as it dwells in Christ bodily. It tells us that "ALL THE BUILDING fitly framed together GROWETH INTO A HOLY TEMPLE in the Lord, in whom ye also are builded together for an habitation of God in the Spirit." It reminds us that "Christ loved the Church and gave Himself up for it, that He might present the Church to Himself a GLORIOUS CHURCH, not having spot or wrinkle, or any such thing." It suggests that all that we know of the close and intimate union between our body and its head with all its members, of the wonderful power that the head has to move and use every member, and the readiness with which every member yields itself to the service of the head on behalf of its fellow members, is but a shadow of that still more mysterious power by which every believer is linked to Christ and ever holds himself at the disposal of his fellow-believers.

"ONE SPIRIT AND BODY." This body of Christ is to be the very highest revelation of the glory of God, manifesting His power to make the creature of the dust, fallen under the power of sin and Satan, the partaker of the likeness and the holiness of the ever-blessed Son. It is the work over which the Holy Spirit presides in this dispensation, as He subordinates all His work in the individual believer to carry out the eternal purpose, that they all should be one, even as the Father is one with the Son. It is only as the Church yields herself to His divine working and makes His great aim her aim too, that the power of the Holy Spirit can be expected to work unhindered either in the Church as a whole, or in the individual members.

The work which this Spirit of Unity is to do we find

in the following verses. When ascended up on high, Christ gave to His Church the gifts of apostles and prophets, evangelists and pastors and teachers "for the perfecting of the saints, unto the work of ministering unto the building up of the Body of Christ." Note well, it is not the apostles and prophets and pastors who are to build up the Body of Christ; their work is the perfecting of the saints for the ministry of building up. Every saint is to be trained and perfected to take his part in the building up of the Body of Christ. Just as every member of my body helps the building up of the whole, every believer is to know his place and work in the Body of Christ, caring for every other member. Each one needs the other; each one is to care for the others; each one is to feel himself so linked to the whole, in the love of the Spirit, that he shall not only avoid and put away everything that is selfish or unloving, but shall actively yield himself to the Spirit to be the instructor and the comforter of all who are weaker.

And then follows—"Till we all attain unto the unity of faith, unto a full grown man, unto the measure of the stature of the fulness of Christ." Nothing less than this is to be the aim of each one, not only for himself but for all around him, that so indeed the body may be the fulness of Him that filleth all in all. Thus alone can we "grow up into Him in all things, which is the Head, even Christ; from Whom all the body, fitly framed and knit together, according to the working in due measure of each several part, maketh the increase of the Body, UNTO THE BUILDING UP OF ITSELF IN LOVE."

The bearing of all this on the spiritual life and our devotions is clear. As long as our prayers only aim at our own perfection and happiness they defeat themselves; the selfishness that is their aim prevents the answer. It is alone in the union with the whole body that each member can be healthy and strong. The building up of the Body in love is indispensable to our spiritual health. Let us see to it that intercession, "with all prayer and supplication, praying at all seasons in the Spirit for all the saints," be the proof that the Spirit of Unity dwells and prays in us. Let us "love the brethren with a pure heart fervently." In our home life, in prayer circles, in all our fellowship with God's children, let our love watch over and encourage them, and ever remember that we and they are indispensable to each other. Let the Spirit of Unity be the life of our secret devotions; grace will be given to live our whole life in unceasing devotion to Christ and His glorious body, unto the building up of itself in love.

XIII

GRIEVING THE SPIRIT

"Grieve not the Holy Spirit of God."—EPH. iv. 30.

WHAT a sad summing up of the history of Israel and of the whole Old Testament Covenant we have in the words of Isaiah: "They vexed His Holy Spirit"; and of Stephen: "Ye do always resist the Holy Ghost; as your fathers did, so do ye." In the New Testament provision was made that this should no longer be the case. God promised to His people a new heart and a new spirit; a heart in which His law was written and into which He put His Spirit, so that they should keep His judgments and do them. The Spirit of God's Son is given so to live in us, and have the mastery over us, that grieving Him should no longer be a necessity. The warning, "Grieve not the Spirit," is a promise; what grace commands it enables us to perform. The believer who seeks to live unceasingly in the consciousness that he has been "sealed with the Holy Spirit," will find, in his faith in the power and presence of that Spirit within him, the assurance that it is possible to live without grieving Him.

And yet the danger is so near and so strong, unless we live entirely under the power of the Spirit, that we need to give heed to the warning, and make a study of all that can by any possibility hinder His blessed work in us. The context (from ver. 25) speaks of falsehood, and anger, and stealing, and corrupt speech, and transgressions of the law of love. These were to be put far away; everything that is against God's law must grieve His Holy Spirit. But there is more. All the commands of the Lord Jesus, through the beatitudes pronounced on the poor in spirit, and the meek, and the merciful, and the pure in heart; through all His teaching as to bearing the cross, denying self, forsaking the world and following Him; down to His last injunctions to His disciples to love one another as He had loved them, to serve one another and each to be least,—are so many marks of the Heavenly life Christ came to bring. Everything that is not in harmony with these must grieve the Spirit and prevent enjoyment of His blessed Presence.

There is still more. When Paul tells us that "what is not of faith is sin," he reminds us how, while God's Word announces the great principles of our action, it leaves to the individual believer under the teaching of the Spirit the application of those principles in daily life. In little things, in doubtful things, in things in regard to which there is a difference among Christians, the believer grieves the Spirit where he does not wait for His guidance, or does not act on what appears to him to be His mind. The whole life is to be under His control with the heart watchful and ready to obey in everything. What is not of faith must be yielded up to God at once, or it may become a cloud that darkens the light of the Spirit in His divine tenderness.

Once more Scripture speaks of the struggle between the flesh and the Spirit, and tells us that the only way in which a believer can live the life in the Spirit is in the power of the truth: "They that are of Christ Jesus have crucified the flesh." That means nothing less than that even as Christ yielded His life and His flesh to the death of the cross, so the believer accepts God's judgment on his whole sinful nature as embodied in the flesh. His own will, his own strength, his goodness have been given up to the power of the cross. He lives by the faith: "I am crucified with Christ, Christ liveth in me." Anything that yields to the flesh, and allows it, instead of being crucified, to have its way, and maintain its life, must, by the very necessity of the case, hinder and grieve the blessed Spirit. Oh! what a tender, humble, watchful dependence upon the blessed Spirit and His leading is needful if we are to maintain His fellowship undisturbed.

Then comes last what is the most important of all. The great work of the Holy Spirit is to reveal Christ to the believer, in the glory of His heavenly life, and in the power by which He actually works in our hearts. As a preparation for this, His first work is to convict of the sin of unbelief. The salvation God has prepared for us is all comprised in Jesus Christ; the life He lived on earth, of humility and obedience, has been prepared for us, and can be received and lived on continuously through simple faith alone. The great secret of the true Christian lies in this one thing: the daily, the unceasing faith in what Jesus is, and has for us, and will most assuredly work in us each moment of our life. It is because this faith is not exercised, is not sought after, that the Christian life is so feeble. There is nothing that grieves the Holy Spirit so much, even in those who have in some measure sought to obtain the victory in other things, as the unbelief by which Jesus is prevented from showing His power and His glory in working out His deliverance from the power of sin and of the world.

Would God that we saw clearly the simplicity and the glory of the Gospel we profess. In Jesus Christ there is stored up for us the new nature, all that by His life and death and resurrection He wrought out; out of this fulness we receive grace for grace. He is the corn of wheat that died; the fulness of life that there is in Himself is reproduced in us, enabling us to grow

into the likeness of His humility and love and obedience.
And this not by any power in ourselves. The Holy
Spirit is given and lives in us to communicate and maintain, just as the air does in our body, the life of Christ
in the soul. Oh! to feel how urgent the command is:
"Grieve not the Spirit of God," and what an unspeak-
able blessing will come if we yield to Him.

We are in search of the New Testament standard of
a life of devotion. What does our text teach in regard
to Paul's thought about it? Could he have answered
one of his readers asking for his experience—"I grieve
and vex the Holy Spirit every day"? Surely not. And
if he could not say this, would he have laid it down
as the rule for others? I cannot think so. To any question he would have answered: I am sure that the child
of God, living fully in the power of the Holy Spirit,
can please God; there is no necessity for his grieving
the Spirit every day.

Is not the different standard of our modern Christianity the simple result of ignorance and unbelief in
regard to the supernatural working of the ever-blessed
Spirit in the heart? Paul lived his life of devotion in
the fulness and the joy of the Holy Ghost. Is not our
standard limited by the fact that such an experience is
but seldom taught and experienced? And is not the
cause of all, that our knowledge is too much that of the
intellect, and that the Holy Spirit is not honoured as
the only Teacher of spiritual truth? We need to return
to the prayer in the first chapter (15–23), and what it
teaches us of the absolute need of receiving from the
Father the gift of the Spirit of Wisdom, as the only
Teacher that can enable us to apprehend and experience
the heavenly life that God has prepared for us.

XIV

FILLED WITH THE SPIRIT

"Be not drunken with wine, but be filled with the Spirit, speaking one to another in psalms and hymns and spiritual songs."

EPH. v. 18, 19.

"GRIEVE not the Spirit!" "Be filled with the Spirit!" In these two injunctions all our duty to the Spirit is included. The one is negative, forbidding everything of the flesh or self that would lead to unbelief or disobedience to Christ Jesus. The other positive, calling us to yield our whole being in undivided surrender to Him Who reveals and maintains the life of Christ within us.

To understand the command: "Be filled with the Spirit," we need only turn to the Day of Pentecost, where the disciples were all "filled with the Holy Spirit." We know what that meant to them. For three years they had lived day and night in closest fellowship with their Lord. His presence had been everything to them. When He spoke of His departure their hearts were sad. He promised that the Spirit would come, not to take His place, but to reveal Himself as their Lord, ever present with them as much as when He was upon earth, only far more intimately and more gloriously. He would henceforth not be near them and beside them, without the power of enabling them to do what He had taught them, but would live and work in them, even as the Father had lived and worked in Him as man. To be filled with the Spirit would mean to them that Christ on the throne would be to them an ever-present living reality, filling their hearts and life with all His heavenly love and joy. Their fellowship with Him on earth would prove to have been but the shadow of that intense and unceasing union with Him, which the Spirit would reveal in power.

The command: "Be filled with the Spirit," is a pledge that all that the disciples received and enjoyed at Pentecost, is indeed, for us too. The Church has sunk down from the level of Pentecost to a life in which the spirit of the world and of human wisdom is, alas, far too prevalent. Few believe in the possibility of the unbroken presence of Christ dwelling in the heart, conquering sin by His holy Presence, inspiring to devotion and perfect self-sacrifice by the fire of His love, guiding each hour into all His will and work by the leading of His blessed Spirit. The heavenly vision of Christ at the right hand of God, ministering, in the power of His infinite redemption, not only salvation to the penitent, but full salvation to all whom He has sanctified by His one offering, is scarcely known. And, as the result of this, there are but few found to witness to "the exceeding greatness of His power toward us who believe".

The condition, too, on which this blessing is to be received cannot be better studied than in the disciples. They had turned their back upon the world, and forsaken all to follow Christ. They had learnt to know and love Him, and do His will. As our Saviour said Himself: "If ye love Me, ye will keep My commandments, and I will pray the Father, and He will give you another Comforter." They had continued with Him in His temptations; He carried them with Him through death and the grave; the joy and the power of the resurrection life filled their hearts with confidence and hope. Their whole being was yielded up and, one might say, lost in the ascended Lord upon the throne,—they were indeed ready, fully prepared, to receive the wondrous gift that was to come upon them.

The Church of our day, how sadly it is lacking in that separation from the world, in that intense attachment and obedience to Christ, in that fellowship with His suffering and conformity to His death, in that devotion to Christ on the throne, and in that confident expectation of the never-ceasing flow of the water of life from under the throne, which gives the assurance that the fulness of the Spirit will not be withheld! No wonder that the mighty power of God is so little known and felt in our church life!

Let us turn once again to Pentecost, and think what the great gift was that was bestowed. Though they knew not at once to say in words what it meant, the Spirit woke in them the consciousness that He, in Whom the Son and the Father had come to dwell in them, was Himself indeed true God, the overflowing fountain, from Whom rivers of life flowed through them, and from them on to the world. Coming fresh from the throne of our Lord in heaven, He rested on them as the Spirit of glory and of God, and filled their hearts with the very love and power of Christ in glory. As the mighty power of God dwelling in them, He convinced the world by their boldness, by their love, that God was indeed in their midst.

How different the conception of most Christians of what the Spirit is, and oh, how different their experience of the presence and the power of Christ that He imparts. How much the thought of the Spirit is little more than a mental conception, or a passing emotion, with its sense of power or of happiness. How little there is of the consciousness that fills the soul with deep reverence and quiet rest, with heavenly joy and strength, as the natural and permanent possession of the life of the believer. The name of the blessed Spirit, twelve times repeated in our Epistle, in all His various graces, marks the character of the life of the primitive Church in contrast with so much of our own time.

"Be filled with the Spirit." This filling has its very great difference in degree, from the first joy of a new but ignorant convert in a revival, through all the experiences by which he is taught what more is needed and is waiting for him, on to being filled with all the fulness of God as that comes through the dwelling of Christ in the heart.

In all filling we know how two things are needed. The one that the vessel be clean and empty and ready, even in its posture, to receive the water that is waiting for it. The other that the water be near and ready to give away itself in full measure to the waiting vessel. In the great transaction between God and man for the filling of the Spirit, man needs first of all to know how complete the surrender is that is needed, and how, even to the death to self and the world, the yielding up of the whole being is indispensable. And then how willing and ready, and oh, so able, the Holy God is to take possession of our being, and to fill it with Himself.

When our Lord Jesus said: "He that believeth on Me, out of him shall flow rivers of living water," He made the one condition of being filled with the Spirit to overflowing, nothing more and nothing less, than simple faith in Himself. Faith is not an imagination, not an argument or an intellectual conviction; it claims the whole heart, it yields up the whole being; it entrusts itself unreservedly to the power that seeks to take possession of it. IT IS IN THE LIFE OF FAITH, CULTIVATED IN SECRET FELLOWSHIP AND ADORING WORSHIP, IN UNCEASING DEPENDENCE AND WHOLE-HEARTED SURRENDER, THAT THE BLESSING WILL BE FOUND.

What a study for our hour's devotion, and what a call

to beseech our blessed Lord to deliver us from all that could keep us back from a life of full faith and close tender fellowship with Himself. What a call to worship and to wait until God the Spirit dwell within us, revealing the Father and the Son, and all that wonderful life of heaven whereby He works in the heart even what is done in heaven above.

XV

THE SWORD OF THE SPIRIT

"Take the sword of the Spirit, which is the word of God."
EPH. vi. 17.

PAUL begins the last section of the Epistle with the words: "Finally, be strong in the Lord, and in the strength of His might." What he had written in chap. i (19) of "the exceeding greatness of God's power in us who believe," even nothing less than the resurrection power by which Christ was lifted to the throne, and again, in chapter iii (16), of our "being strengthened with power through the Spirit in the inner man," he meant in very deed to be the experience of these believers. They are to prove in their lives that all that has been said of God's power to manifest itself in His Church is a Divine reality. The Spirit is the mighty power of God; the Spirit-filled Christian is to be strong for God's service and the wars of His kingdom. He tells them that they are not "wrestling with flesh and blood, but against the principalities and powers and world-rulers of darkness, and spiritual hosts of wickedness in the heavenly places," and warns them that nothing less will do than to live every day with the whole armour of God on them, standing strong in Christ and in the strength of His might. The believer has not only to meet the single evil spirits that tempt him, but is to regard himself as one of the host whom Christ leads to warfare against the kingdom of darkness in all its forms, to win the world back for its King and Lord. In the work of the Church the victory of the Cross over the power of Satan is to be carried out in that same power in which Christ triumphed over the grave.

When Paul says, "Take up the whole armour of God," he begins by speaking of the various parts of defensive armour. The Christian first of all needs to see that at every point of his whole being he be personally safe in the protection of his Lord. Then alone is he fit for acting on the offensive. Paul mentions only one weapon of attack—the sword. And that sword is the Sword of the Spirit, the Word of God.

To know its power and how to use it effectually, we have but to look to our leader, the Captain of the Lord's host. When Jesus Christ met Satan in the wilderness, He conquered him by the Word of God alone. As man He had studied that Word, He had loved it, He had obeyed it, He had lived in it. The Holy Spirit, through Whom He was driven to the wilderness, found in Him the familiar words with which he could meet and conquer every Satanic suggestion. To take the sword of the Spirit in the hour of battle means that I have lived in that Word, and had it abiding in me; that I have lived it out, and so given it the mastery of my whole being, that the Spirit of Christ within me can enable me in the power of faith to cast out Satan by it. It is the man who yields up his whole being to the Word, who "lives by every word that proceedeth out of the mouth of God," who will be a good soldier of Jesus Christ. Whether in the struggle with infidelity and worldliness, with open sin or secret iniquity, with feeble, hopeless Christians, with dark superstition or nominal Christianity, or a back-sliding Church, or still darker heathenism—the Word of God will always and everywhere be the weapon of victory to those who know how to use it aright.

Who know how to use it aright! What that means we learn from the vision of John in Patmos, when he saw One like unto the Son of Man, and "out of His mouth went a sharp two-edged sword. And afterwards heard Him speak, "These things saith He that hath the sharp two-edged sword! Repent, or else I will come unto thee quickly, and will war against thee with the sword of my mouth." It is when Christ has been revealed to us, calling us to repent of every sin, and above all, of the sin of our unbelief, and has warred against us, and the evil in us, with the sword of His mouth, that the power of the Word will be revealed in us, and we shall be strong to wield it as the sword of the Spirit. "For the Word of God is living and active, and sharper than any two-edged sword, piercing even to the dividing of soul and spirit" (showing on the one hand all that is soulish or natural, and that which is spiritual and divine), "and is quick to discern the thoughts and intents of the heart," discovering our most secret intentions and inclinations in the light of God and His holiness. It is the branch that has thus been cleansed through the Word that will bear much fruit. The soul that has fully yielded itself to the sword of His mouth will have faith and strength to wield it against every enemy.

Every believer is meant to be a soldier in Christ's army. The spiritual powers of darkness are to be met and overcome by all who have learned that they have not been saved for their own sakes alone, that they are not to live to themselves, but wholly for Him who bought them. From Heaven He leads them as His conquering hosts, to rout the spiritual hosts of wickedness in heavenly places. Alas, that there are so many Christians who have never understood their calling, and have never yet given their lives unreservedly for the one object of securing the triumph of our Redeemer in the world!

Let us listen to the summons that calls us to the war. Let us confess and repent that we have so little stood in the strength of the Lord, and in the power of His might, with our armour on day and night. Let our ears be opened to the calls that comes from every Church for men and women who will yield themselves to Christ for His service, whether in the home or the foreign field. Let us remember that it is first of all in our own life that we are to prove the power that God's Word has with Himself in prayer and intercession, and with ourselves in surrender and cleansing. It is there we learn to use it. It is there the love to our Lord and the love to our souls will rouse us to the war. It is there that the Word of God will in very deed become the Sword of the Spirit, that we ever carry girded on our thigh, ready to meet the enemy and to deliver his captives. How helpless is the Church of our day with its twenty thousand missionaries to meet the needs of one thousand million heathen and Mohammedans. And how strong it might be if every believer were to be trained to yield himself to the sharp two-edged sword proceeding out of the mouth of the Son of Man, and when it has done its work in himself, to grasp it, and with it carry deliverance to those who are dying in such sore bondage.

God forgive us that our devotions have so often been the vain attempt to find nourishment or joy in the Word of God. We failed because our first thought was the selfish one of seeking comfort or holiness for ourselves. Let us repent and learn that a Christian in seeking salvation is to be brought to Christ that Christ may use him as a member of His body for the welfare of the whole, of those, too, who have not yet been gathered into it. And let our devotions henceforth bear these two simple marks—the entire surrender to the Word of God as the two-edged sword, dividing soul and spirit; the surrender to wield that two-edged sword in the faith of the power of God's Holy Spirit against every enemy of Christ and His Kingdom. What light and blessing can then come to our hours of devotion.

XVI

THE SPIRIT OF PRAYER

"With all prayer and supplication, praying at all seasons in the Spirit, and watching thereunto in all perseverance and supplication for all the saints, and on my behalf."—EPH. vi. 18.

THE words are connected with the whole preceding context: Be strong in the Lord, put on the whole armour of God. Our wrestling is against the spiritual hosts of wickedness in the heavenly places. Stand, therefore, putting on the whole armour of God, both defensive and offensive, WITH ALL PRAYER AND SUPPLICATION, PRAYING AT ALL SEASONS IN THE SPIRIT. The Christian's power, the Christian's wrestling, his putting on his armour, and his wielding the sword of the Spirit, is all to be in the unceasing dependence upon God, and the believing confidence in His all-sufficient grace. A life of unceasing prayer is the secret of a life of victory. PRAYING ALWAYS IN THE SPIRIT IS THE MARK OF THE NORMAL SPIRITUAL LIFE.

This praying at all seasons is to be in the Spirit. As unceasingly as my lungs are kept breathing, and my heart beating by the Divine power which upholds my physical life, so continually and most certainly will the Holy Spirit breathe in me that prayer by which the powers of the Divine life and of the heavenly world are maintained. Salvation is not by works, or effort, or struggling. I am God's workmanship, created in Christ Jesus unto good works, which God afore prepared that we should walk in them; a divine creation not finished and left to itself, but with my life moment by moment upheld by the Word of His power. Unceasing prayer is possible, is commanded, BECAUSE THE ETERNAL SPIRIT EVER WORKS IT AS THE HEAVENWARD BREATHING OF THE SOUL. "With all prayer and supplication, praying at all seasons in the Spirit."

But this praying at all seasons is by no means selfish, with its reference only to our own needs: "Watching thereunto in all perseverance and supplication for all the saints." In the Epistle Paul has taught us the large place that the truth of the Body of Christ in its unity in love (see chap. ii. 13–22; chap. iii. 6, 18; chap. iv. 1–16; chap. v. 22–33) takes in the Gospel. As he has spoken of the wrestling to which believers are called with the powers of darkness, he speaks here of the unity of the saints forming one great army as the host of the Lord, animated by one Spirit, and all striving together for the establishment of His kingdom in the world. CONTINUAL EARNEST PRAYER FOR ALL BELIEVERS is not only the duty of each one, but that on which the welfare and the victory of the whole depends.

What specially we are to pray for the saints we can learn from Paul's own petitions. Look back to chap. i. 15–23, and its plea on behalf of those who had already been sealed with the Spirit, that He would give them the Spirit of wisdom and divine illumination that they might know THE EXCEEDING GREATNESS OF HIS POWER in all who believe. Oh, how believers need that this great truth should get a place in their hearts, and thoroughly possess them! And how believers who have sought this for themselves need to be reminded of their calling to send up this prayer for others. The health of the Church as a whole, the spiritual strength of individual believers or Churches, depends more than we can think upon the unceasing watching in all perseverance and supplication for all the saints. And study with this the prayer in chap. iii. 14–21, where Paul, as he bows his knees, cries to God to grant something special "according to the riches of His glory." That these sealed believers MIGHT BE STRENGTHENED WITH DIVINE POWER, that so they may be filled with all the fulness of God. Do let us take in the thought. True believers stand greatly in need of the prayers of all to whom the Spirit of supplication is given. The prayer is to be definite and pointed, pleading for the Spirit of Divine power to fill their whole inner man, that Christ may dwell in their hearts, and they be rooted in love. All believers are to unite in pleading for all the saints that God may make all this true in them.

And such prayer is to be a watching thereunto with all perseverance. PRAYING ALWAYS IN THE SPIRIT FOR ALL saints will be the secret of true revival in God's children. AND ON MY BEHALF! The minister who is pleading as intercessor for the saints whom he watches over HAS EQUAL NEED OF THEIR PRAYERS IN RETURN. As the life-blood which is ever purified by the fresh air we breathe circulates through the whole body and maintains its unity in vital power, even so the Spirit of prayer, breathing in the air of heaven, and breathing out and up to heaven the unceasing supplication of love on behalf of the whole body and every member, is essential to the health of the body of Christ. The work of the ministry depends upon it. The minister is to train believers to this as one of their highest privileges. The work of the missionary who, like Paul, carries the gospel to the heathen, depends upon it. Oh, that we believed in the new power that could come upon our Missions if believers answered the call "praying at all seasons in the Spirit, and watching thereunto in all perseverance and supplication on my behalf." What grace would come in answer! "To make known with boldness the mystery of the Gospel," and to preach, whether to the wise or to the ignorant, to the Greek or the Jew, to the follower of Mohammed or of dumb idols, Christ a stumbling-block to the Jew and foolishness to the Gentiles—Christ, the power of God and the wisdom of God.

What a vision of the work to be done in our daily hour of devotion. A vision of the hosts of spiritual wickedness in heavenly places, of Jesus Christ holding rule over all, and carrying out the triumph of the Cross, and of ministers and members of Christ labouring together and wrestling in preaching and in praying for the conquest of the world. Oh, what a new meaning and glory our devotions would have, if with a life in the Spirit as He has been revealed to us in this Epistle, a life strong in the Lord AND THE EXCEEDING GREATNESS OF HIS STRENGTH WITHIN US, we live no longer to ourselves and our selfish religious hopes and efforts, but live in love, even as Christ loved us, and each gives himself a sacrifice and an offering to God for the building up of the Body of Christ.

May God help us to catch the inspiration of the true standard of life the Epistle has held out to us, and to believe with an undoubting confidence that God will make it true, even to a life praying always in the Spirit, and watching thereunto for all the saints, and above all, for the ministers of the Gospel.

CONCLUSION

XVII

A REVIEW

"God hath blessed us with every spiritual blessing in heavenly places in Christ."—EPH. i. 3.

I N our Epistle the expression, "the heavenly places," is used five times. IN THEM, God hath blessed us with every spiritual blessing in Christ; He hath set Christ at His own right hand; He hath made us sit with Christ; the manifold wisdom of God is to be made known through the Church to principalities and powers; we are to be fitted for wrestling against the spiritual hosts of wickedness. The life of the Christian is regarded in its spiritual and heavenly aspect; he cannot live it except in the power of the heavenly world.

The Epistle has been called The Alps of the New Testament. As one peak rises above another, so the Apostle delights to lead us through the heavenly truths of election and redemption, of the mystery of God's will and His purpose in Christ, of our resurrection and ascension with Christ, our new creation and all our glory as the Body of Christ. And as the light of the Holy Spirit shines upon one truth after another, we learn how truly divine and heavenly our life on earth can be.

We have studied the twelve passages in which the Holy Spirit is mentioned. Let us now seek to gather all their teaching into one, and see if we can frame a picture of the man called to live by this heavenly standard.

1. The sealing of the Spirit. The believer has been sealed in Christ, and into Him, by the Holy Spirit of promise, the earnest of his inheritance, the pledge of what he is and can become in Christ, the divine assurance that every promise can be made true. He has the seal of God upon his forehead; his whole being bears the stamp of the Holy Spirit.

2. The first great grace of the Spirit is that He enlightens our eyes to know aright what we have been called to by God, and what the exceeding greatness of God's power is to enable us to live worthy of that calling. The Holy Spirit reveals the working of the might of God's power in raising Christ from the dead to the throne of glory, as the pledge of what God will each day work in us.

3. The sealed one, brought nigh by the blood, lives in the Holy Place, lives through the Spirit a life of perfect and abiding access to God in Christ Jesus.

4. The sealed one no longer lives for himself, but as a member of the great spiritual temple built for an habitation of God through the Spirit. The Spirit links him to the chief cornerstone and to all his fellow saints.

5. The sealed one knows the mystery of Christ among the Gentiles, and counts them as fellow heirs, to whom all the unsearchable riches of Christ are to be made known. He lives for the Kingdom and the ingathering of the heathen as Christ's inheritance.

6. The sealed one ever learns that it is only by the direct interposition of an almighty power that he can live his life in the heavenly places. He ever returns to pray that the power of the Spirit may strengthen him mightily, that Christ may dwell in his heart by faith, and he with all the saints may be filled with love and with all the fulness of God. He asks for nothing less for

himself and for others than that God in his infinite power may reveal His Son in them.

7. The sealed one bears the mark of the likeness of Jesus, the meek and lowly one. He walks worthy of his heavenly calling, in all lowliness and meekness maintaining the unity of the Spirit unbroken. He knows that he can do this because God strengthens him with might in the inner man.

8. The sealed one knows that there is one body and one spirit, and that his one calling is to live for the work of ministering to the saints in building up the Body of Christ in love.

9. The sealed one seeks above everything never to grieve the Holy Spirit of God. How should he dare to break the seal that God has set upon him, the Spirit of a holy life? It is only thus that he can partake of all the blessings in the heavenly places in Christ. He cultivates a tender spirit.

10. "Be filled with the Spirit." The more the believer knows the blessedness of the sealing of the Spirit and all the work that He does, all the more the desire awakens to yield himself in utter emptiness to His control. At the same time he feels the need of a deeper vision of the riches of that grace which the blessed Spirit is given to dispense. He sees that to be filled with the Spirit means nothing else than peace and joy and health and strength.

11. The sealing of the Spirit includes the calling to be a soldier, and to be strong in the Lord and the power of His might. The believer begins to understand why such divine power is promised him. It is that with the Sword of the Spirit he may wrestle against the powers of evil, and rescue men for Christ and His service.

12. The sealed ones know to obey the call to a life of continual prayer, watching thereunto with all perseverance for all saints, and for all ministers of the Word.

The Spirit makes it possible for them to be true soldiers and prayer warriors.

"Blessed be the God and Father of our Lord Jesus, Who has blessed us with all spiritual blessings in heavenly places in Christ!" Let us think of the twelve-fold blessing until we realise what a salvation God has prepared for us. A believer sealed by the Spirit, taught by the Spirit to know the divine power working in him, kept in the full consciousness of perfect and abiding access to the Father, united with all his fellow saints in the one temple as the habitation of God, led into the mystery of Christ among the Gentiles, strengthened with might by the Spirit in the inner man to own Christ dwelling in the heart, and to be filled with all the fulness of God. And then, coming down into his everyday life, he walks in all meekness and lowliness, keeping the unity of the Spirit, and in the power of that Spirit ministers to the building up of the Body in love; seeking never to grieve the Spirit, but ever to be filled with Him, he fulfils the law of love in all his daily life, he is strong in the Lord and the power of His might to fulfil his destiny in wrestling with the powers of darkness, in the use of the Word, and prayer for all saints.

It needs time, and thought, and prayer, and above all, quiet waiting on the Spirit of God for anyone to get the vision, and to keep it, of the Spirit-sealed, Spirit-taught, Spirit-strengthened, Spirit-filled believer as here set before us. It needs a turning away from self and the world to allow God to work in us all His purpose according to the counsel of His own will.

And let us not forget the purpose with which we undertook the study of the Epistle. Let us believe in the Divine standard of the Christian life it sets before us. Let us believe in the almighty power of God, by which alone, but most surely, it can become ours.

Let us believe that if we are in earnest in seeking deliverance from the carnal standard, we can count upon the infinite mercy of God to work in us what otherwise appears to be utterly hopeless—a life filled with the Spirit.

XVIII

BECAUSE OF UNBELIEF

"Why could not we cast it out? And He saith unto them, Because of your little faith."—MATT. xvii. 19, 20.

IN connection with our last chapter, I could almost wish that it were possible to have a Referendum from all my readers in answer to the question, as to whether they think it possible to carry out the Ephesian standard of the spiritual life in their own daily practice. Not a few would be found to say that they do not see how it can be possible in view of the truth, held by universal consent, as to the remnant of sin in every believer, making the daily confession of sin an absolute necessity. Others might answer that though, to a man like Paul, and those whom he calls spiritual men, such a standard is possible, yet it is not within reach of all; such a life is not for them. And a large majority would content themselves with the thought of a beautiful and attractive ideal, which, though not within our reach, exercises its stimulating and elevating influence even on those who remain far below it.

And yet the more I study the Epistle, the deeper the conviction grows: Surely Paul meant in all sincerity to testify of what God had not only shown as by revelation, but had actually wrought within him. He speaks in chapter i not only of the revelation of the Spirit to make us know "the exceeding greatness of God's power," through our faith in Christ raised from the dead and seated on the throne, but in chapter iii of our being "mightily strengthened by the Spirit in the inner man," so that the great miracle of grace is perfected in us: Christ dwelling in the heart, filling us with all the fulness of God. And when he adds the ascription of praise, "To Him that is able to do exceeding abundantly above all that we can ask or think, according to the power that worketh in us, to Him be glory for ever and ever," he undoubtedly means that this was his own experience, and he confidently urges his readers to believe that it can be theirs. The exceeding greatness of God's power working in the heart from moment to moment, day by day, is the ground on which the standard of devotion rests, which he holds out to us. But it needs—his two great prayers prove this—it needs special and unceasing prayer to know this power, to believe it, to receive it. Without this it is nothing but natural to us to regard the standard as an impracticable one, and so to continue in ignorance of what is offered for our acceptance.

The question may be asked: But how comes it that in the Church of Christ this mighty power of God working in us is so little taught, and so little experienced? Is, then, the whole Church in error in its resting content with a far lower standard than what this Epistle holds out to us? The answer to this question will lead us to the very root of the evil from which the Church is suffering.

We all know how God gave Abraham to Israel as the great example of faith in Him, counting as he did that God was able even to quicken the dead, both in his own case and in the sacrifice of Isaac. Yet we know too how Israel, from the very commencement of God's dealings in Egypt, continually grieved Him by unbelief, until at length, through that unbelief, it was condemned to forty years' wanderings in the wilderness. And onward through the years, as Psalm lxxviii tells us, "they continually limited Him by unbelief." We know, too, how our Lord Jesus continually sought to cultivate in His disciples the habit of faith as the one condition for their seeing the power and the glory of God. And when later on He made Paul the last of the Apostles, He set him forth as a witness to the power of faith, not only in justification, BUT IN THE WHOLE OF OUR SPIRITUAL LIFE AND SERVICE. And yet just as Israel, notwithstanding the example of Abraham, utterly failed of trusting God, so in the Church of Christ it became manifest all too speedily how little man knows to receive his salvation on trust in God alone. We know how terribly the Galatians failed; how the Epistle to the Hebrews warns above everything against unbelief; and how speedily the Church of the second century was brought into bondage under the law. The whole Romish Church, in its first origins, is a proof of how naturally the human heart turns from grace and faith to law and works.

In the lives of the Church Fathers we find, with all their earnestness, how little they understood of faith in the power of God as the one secret of a life in His will. And so they came to cultivate a religion in which the grace of God was ever connected with the confession of much sinning, while the tone of Paul and his faith in God's mighty keeping and saving power was little heard. The generations to which the Reformation brought the Gospel of Justification by Faith little understood that Sanctification is as much by faith, and that the power of a holy life for victory over the world and the flesh is nowhere to be found but IN AN IMMEDIATE AND UNCEASING EXERCISE OF FAITH IN THE EXCEEDING GREATNESS OF GOD'S POWER TO USWARD. And so in the Church of our day it need not be wondered at that one of the great causes of its feebleness is—the unbelief in the mighty power of Jesus.

One often hears complaints of the lack of power in

the Church, both to guide its members to true devotion to Christ and the service of His kingdom, and really to influence the unsaved masses around us. Many are the causes that are sometimes mentioned, but the chief cause of all is too little considered—a Church THAT DOES NOT EXPERIENCE AND WITNESS TO THE POWER OF CHRIST DWELLING IN THE HEARTS OF HIS PEOPLE TO OVERCOME THE POWER OF SIN cannot expect that mighty power in its conflict with Satan and his hosts. The first great work of the Holy Spirit is to convince of unbelief. Where that work has not been fully done, nothing will avail until the Church is brought to confess that all its feebleness is owing to this one thing, its not giving Christ His place of honour. "All power in heaven and on earth is given to Me"; as the Church believes and experiences this she will learn to expect Him to do His mighty works.

Let me once again urge every reader who has followed me thus far to ask himself the question: Do I believe in the power of God in Christ by His Spirit to work in me the life depicted in this Epistle? Instead of ever again mourning over the sins that we cannot master, the pride, or the self-will, or the lack of love, or the short-coming in obedience to all God's will, let us at once come to the root of the matter, and confess the terrible sin of our unbelief in "the exceeding greatness of God's power" revealed in Christ, and in that "strengthening by the Spirit with might" which leads us on to the fulness of God. As we yield ourselves to the Holy Spirit to bring us low before God in the confession of our unbelief, He will so reveal Christ in us that our life can indeed become the response to the divine call: "Be strong in the Lord and in the power of His might."

XIX

POSSIBLE WITH GOD

"Who then can be saved? But He said, The things which are impossible with men are possible with God."—LUKE xviii. 26, 27.

IF the great hindrance to the power of God's Word in the truth that we have found in Ephesians be the thought, "the standard is an impossible one," our own resource must be ever again to listen to the voice of Christ as He tells us that what is impossible with man is in very deed possible to God. God can do for us what appears to be utterly beyond His reach and ours. God can, not only by the Holy Spirit, work in us what He wrought in Paul, and gave him to teach us, but God can also, by His Spirit, work in us the blessed confidence that He will do it for us. Let us, ere we part from our Epistle, just think what is implied in the great gift of the Holy Spirit.

There is no word that is used in such a variety of meanings as the word "spirit". From anything in which the mind of man exerts and proves its power, to the very highest revelation of God's holiness and love, the same word has to do service, exposed to the danger of each one understanding it according to his point of view. And so within the sphere of Bible truth we often suffer from our very partial and defective view of what is really meant by the Spirit of God and of Christ. Let us try to realise what God means when He promises us the Spirit of Christ.

When God sent His Son into the world in our nature

it was that He might work out in His life a holy nature and disposition, which might be imparted to him who believes in Christ as a thing already prepared and brought into existence for us. When Christ died, it was that He might lay down His life, and then, just as the grain of wheat dies and reappears in the full ear of corn with its hundred-fold reproduction of the seed, live again in our lives here upon earth. To this end the Father gave Him, when He ascended to the throne, the Spirit to pour down as His own life in the heart of His people. "God gave us the Spirit of His Son, crying, Abba Father." The Spirit communicates the holy nature and tempers of Christ with a divine power to all who believe, and in such measure as they believe. They live by the Spirit and are led by the Spirit; the Spirit is their life.

In the wonderful union of the Divine and the human life in the believer everything depends on the true relationship being maintained between God, working all in all, and man receiving all from God to work it out in trust and obedience. Where this is not understood, man is ever ready with his efforts to take the place which God Himself would fill. He thinks that if by earnest prayer he can secure God's help in his efforts, he has found the path to holiness and to growth. He does not understand how the place of the Spirit must be one of absolute and entire control, and his own place that of direct and unceasing dependence. It can be easily seen how two men may be praying the same prayer, that God would give them the Spirit of wisdom or of power, and that the one may be thinking only of such ordinary measures of help as he has connected with the thought of the Spirit, the other is expecting nothing less than that God will do for him above what he can ask or think.

The great secret of the Christian life is to be found in that ceasing from self, in that being brought to nought by the cross of Christ, in which the power of Christ's death manifests itself in us. We all know how our Lord Jesus, ere He could receive the new life from the Father in glory, and the gift of the Holy Spirit through which He could impart His life to His people, had first to give up the life He had lived upon earth. He had to take His place among the dead in utter weakness and helplessness ere He could live again by the power of God. His death on the cross was indispensable to the life of the Spirit. And as it was with Christ, so it must be with us. As we yield ourselves to be united with Him in the likeness of His death, we can share with Him in the glory and power of the life of the Spirit. To know what the Holy Spirit means, implies the knowing of what death means. The cross and the Spirit are inseparable. The soul that understands that the death to self is in Christ the gate to true life, is in the right way to learn what and who the Holy Spirit is.

We shall not have far to seek for the reason why the current conception of what the Holy Spirit can and will do for us is so low. As the great mark of the Pentecostal Church was the presence of the Holy Spirit in power, the great mark of the Church of today is the feeble Spirit workings that are almost everywhere to be found. Our conversions, our preaching, our fellowship, our life, our aggressive work for God and His Kingdom, —everywhere there is the admission that the Spirit in power is but seldom known. While there are endless discussions and efforts for lifting our Christian Churches to a higher level, and for bringing the masses to acknowledge and accept of the truth of God's Word, there has not yet been, on the part of the Church as a whole, anything like what is needed of the intense and sorrowful confession that, as Churches and Christians, we have grieved the Spirit of God. Yes, even we, whose calling it was to honour Him, and to prove by His presence in our life that Christ is indeed Lord, from whom we have received what the world can see and hear in us.

In the Epistle to the Ephesians the Holy Spirit takes a large, a most important place. Paul must have had some reason for thus writing, saturating, as it were, the whole with the truth of the Spirit's presence and work. The Epistle to the Colossians was written about the same time, and bears very many tokens of a common origin in the state of Paul's mind. And yet there is one very marked difference. In Colossians the Holy Spirit is mentioned but once, in Ephesians twelve times, and that in each of his chapters,—one might almost say in every section. It is as if he felt the need of giving expression to a system of truth in which, next to the "in Christ," which occurs some twenty times, the presence and power of the Holy Spirit in the life of the Christian should be specially set forth. We might have had the Epistle without the mention of the Spirit. Those under the full power of the Spirit would have known to supply the omission. But what a loss to the majority of readers! Let us thank God for the gift, and seek to link the truth of the spiritual blessings to the living Spirit, through whom they all come.

Let us, above all, see that when we think of the Holy Spirit we mean WHAT GOD MEANS. He means the Holy Spirit, God the Spirit, God the Holy One, God in His holiness living within us. The more we yield ourselves to this thought, the clearer will become our conceptions of two great truths. The one, that in Him we have the whole God, not only His power, but the living God Himself. The other, that for Him we need the whole man, spirit, soul, and body, to be possessed and controlled by Him. As these two truths master us, and we think of what God in the Spirit is willing to do in us, we shall feel that nothing can keep Him from doing His work in us, but something in ourselves. We shall feel that our great need is to get rid of ourselves, to lose our life, and die with Christ, that the new nature quickened in Him may be the fit vessel for all the blessing the Spirit will bring.

XX

UNTO HIM BE GLORY

"Now unto Him that is able to do exceeding abundantly above a l that we ask or think, according to the power that worketh in us, unto Him be glory."—EPH. iii, 20, 21.

I FEEL as if there is still one point on which I have not pressed as strongly as I should have done. It is the place which the power of God takes in the Epistle, and is meant to take in the life of the Christian. I feel as if I had failed in bringing the reader under the full impression of how all that we have learnt about the Holy Spirit cannot have its full effect without a very special and entire surrender to the almighty working of God's power, and a very intense, personal, and abiding faith that that power must be known and honoured as the one secret of a life according to the New Testament standard. I beseech God to give us the enlightening of His Spirit that we may know "the exceeding greatness of His power in us who believe."

It is remarkable what prominence Paul gives to the thought of our whole salvation being the direct working of God's Almighty power. In chap. i (11) he speaks of "the purpose of Him WHO WORKETH ALL THINGS after the counsel of His will." God does this, not only with regard to the great work of deliverance wrought in Christ, but equally in every detail in the daily life of the Christian. We too often think of Him as the omnipotent One, able to work mightily where He sees occasion. But the words suggest something far greater; He is the God Who works unceasingly, every moment, not only in nature, moment by moment, with its every leaf and flower, but in His children too, all that they need for carrying out His blessed will.

The reader knows the words in the prayer in chap. i: "The exceeding greatness of His power in us who believe." Paul teaches his readers that nothing less than the power of His might that raised Christ from the dead can suffice for the daily need of your soul, and can effect and carry out in you what God has purposed and what He longs to see in you. And it is not until the Holy Spirit brings you to the spiritual insight into "the exceeding greatness of His power to usward who believe," and enables you to carry it about with you as the habitual consciousness of what God is working in you, that God will be able to do for you what He has hitherto not done.

The Christian is so accustomed to strive after the life that the Word puts before him, with the prayer that God would aid him in his weakness, that he has very little conception of how it is alone "the exceeding greatness of God's power" in him that can do the work. "The weakness of God is stronger than man." The strength of God is only to be found in the consciousness of utter weakness. This was the mark of the working of the might of His power in Christ. Our Lord died, sinking down into absolute weakness, without a vestige of the power of thought or of will. He had yielded Himself utterly to the Father, and God's power raised Him out of that absolute weakness to the place of power on the throne. It is alone the teaching of the Holy Spirit that can enable us literally to know this exceeding greatness of God's power working in us.

As this thought masters us we shall get a right conception of what the standard is of the life that Paul puts before us. It is the thought of what God absolutely, by a divine power, will work in us that will give us the courage to see and to accept a life in everything pleasing to Him.

In chap. iii (ver. 7) Paul speaks of the grace of God given him "by the effectual working of His power." He appears to have experienced and to have counted upon this direct working of God in all the grace he needed for his ministry. So he says in Colossians: "I labour, striving according to His working, which worketh in me mightily." The man who believes that will cease from seeking aught in himself; his whole attitude will be that of simple dependence and perfect trust.

The more we strive to take in these thoughts the better we shall understand why, at the close of chap. iii, Paul again returns to the thought of God's almighty power. In chap. i he had spoken of the Spirit's enlightenment to show us how really the power that raised Christ is needed to work in us in every moment and every action of our spiritual life. In chap. iii he goes further, and prays that "the exceeding greatness of God's power," "according to the riches of His glory"—oh, to take time and think what that means!—may be given us as an actual strengthening with might by His Spirit in the inner man. That must mean nothing less than that the whole spiritual life be permanently quickened with such divine power that the indwelling of Christ in the heart, personal, conscious, and abiding, shall be a divine reality. The Church has almost lost the thought of the indwelling of Christ as a continual experience. Before this can become part of our living faith and experience we must learn to look upon the exceeding greatness of God's power, according to the working of His mighty power when He raised Christ from the dead, as part of the inheritance of every

Christian, of which the Holy Spirit is the earnest and the pledge.

To show how full Paul's mind was of the thought of the divine power, as the one condition of the full spiritual life, the doxology which he adds gives God glory just for this one thing—that He is able to do, not only what has just been spoken of, but "exceeding abundantly above all that we ask or think." There are other attributes of God, His love, His righteousness, His holiness, for which we bless His name. But we need to be reminded that, as the groundwork of all, His almighty power must ever be our one confidence in all that He is to do in us in carrying out His purpose. Let us take time, and worship, and adore—"Now unto Him be glory"—until every thought of what is to be done in us, and in the Church, and in the world, is summed up in the one word: "Able to do exceeding abundantly above what we ask or think." "According to the power that worketh in us!"

Just one word more. In this last section (6–10) Paul returns to this thought, and closes all his instruction in the Epistle with the conclusion: "Finally, my brethren, be strong in the Lord, and IN THE POWER OF HIS MIGHT." The very same word which he had used of the raising of Christ (i. 19), "according to the working of the MIGHT OF HIS POWER"; and (iii. 16) "to be STRENGTHENED WITH MIGHT in the inner man." That was meant to be the standard of devotion in those Ephesian Christians. That will become the standard of our devotion when first we learn to cast all our weakness at His feet, and begin to believe with child-like confidence and assurance in the exceeding greatness of His power toward us. We shall gird ourselves for a life strong in the Lord and in the power of His might.

NOTES

CHAPTER VI

1. "But I thought that they had the Spirit already! Yes, certainly; but here is a further gift of the Spirit, a deeper draught. The blessed stream of the Holy Ghost is forever proceeding from the Father and the Son. There is no finality in this work. It is not like Christ's work—a finished work. Observe there is no expression in Scripture which limits the power or the measure of the outgoing of the Holy Ghost. There is no word to say that the Spirit of God is come to an individual or a Church, and that therefore the door may be shut because there is no more Spirit of God to come. We are to be ever receiving, and ever expending, and yet ever expecting at the same time. We must be for evermore opening our hearts to receive further gifts and provisions, for ever letting in great waves of the Spirit to pour through our life. May our God flood us all afresh with fuller waves of truth, and love, and power."—Rev. C. A. Fox, *The Spiritual Grasp of the Epistles*.

2. The Spirit was needed to give A FULLER KNOWLEDGE of God Himself. The word used in Greek is specially significant, implying intimate spiritual apprehension. Then follow three great things into which a spiritual insight is needed for the full Christian life. (1) What the hope of His calling—the knowledge of what the hope was which God held out to them when He called them. In ver. 4 Paul had said, "He chose us that we should be holy and without blemish before Him in love." What light shines upon these words, when the Holy Spirit shows us what possibilities they imply, and how God Himself will make them true in us so as to fit us to be holy to Him for His service on earth in love to all.

(2) "What the riches of the glory of His inheritance in the saints." There is a twofold inheritance. We are God's

heritage. It is of this we read in ver. 11, "In Christ also we were made an heritage." And God is our heritage. Of this we read in ver. 14, "The Holy Spirit is an earnest of our inheritance." "The riches of the glory of His inheritance in the saints," which the Holy Spirit is to reveal, includes both. The words in Colossians (i. 27) show us that this means nothing less than Christ in us, "the riches of the glory of this mystery, which is Christ in you, the hope of glory." Christ is God's treasure, dwelling in our heart with all His unsearchable riches.

(3) "The exceeding greatness of His power to usward, who believe, according to the working of the strength of His might which He wrought in Christ when He raised Him from the dead." This "exceeding greatness of God's power, which He wrought in Christ," remains an enigma, a mystery until the Holy Spirit reveals it by renewing us in the spirit of our mind to see, to desire, and to believe it.

These three great spiritual blessings constitute the sum of what a believer needs to know, and needs the Holy Spirit to teach him. A sight, first of all, of all that God wants him to be. Then a consciousness of the wonderful riches and glory of this inheritance in His saints, nothing less than Christ in them. And then the living assurance that the Almighty power of Christ's resurrection life is actually and unceasingly working in them, to fit them for all that they are to be and to do for God.

Would God that His children believed in the Glory of this mystery, and in the power with which it would work in them, and learned to wait for the Spirit of divine wisdom to reveal it to them.

3. The lessons of this passage for those who are in the ministry, or have charge of souls, are simply invaluable.

They point to the three great spiritual blessings that include all that a Christian needs to know of what God has prepared for him.

They remind us that to preach these truths to believers is not sufficient; human wisdom cannot grasp them.

If the knowledge is to be vital and effectual, it needs a special illumination of the Holy Spirit making us spiritual men. It is only the spiritual man who can discover spiritual things.

It is God Himself, the Father of glory, Who can and will give the Spirit of wisdom, in answer to definite and persevering prayer.

It is the teacher, who has learnt all this for himself, and seeks to bring it home to others, on whom the duty specially devolves of unceasing prayer that God would bestow the gift of the Spirit of wisdom on all to whom the teaching comes.

Such teaching and such praying will lead believers to the full life which the Epistle sets before them.

Let all ministers of the Gospel study and pray this prayer until every thought of preaching or teaching, of the needs of individuals or of all God's children together, is ever borne upward with the supplication, "Father of Glory, give Thy children the Spirit of wisdom and divine revelation in the knowledge of Thyself and all Thou art prepared to work in them."

CHAPTER X

"*That Christ may dwell in your hearts by faith.*" In speaking of his conversion Paul says, "It was the good pleasure of God to REVEAL HIS SON in me that I might preach Him among the Gentiles." In our passage he tells us that this, his own experience, was the very sum and substance of his gospel. When he preached the unsearchable riches of Christ, he preached Him as dwelling in the heart. He would have none of his readers be without it. Without ceasing he pleaded with God to strengthen them with might in their whole inner life, that nothing might keep them from this wonderful blessing.

In a sermon on "Christ in the heart," Dr. M'Laren has said that it is as if the Church has lost the thought of Christ's indwelling being an experience for which Christians ought to seek. And yet how entirely Paul's teaching is in harmony with that of our blessed Lord. In the last night, when He had spoken of the gift of the Holy Spirit, He said: "At that day ye shall know that I am in My Father and ye in Me, and I IN YOU." He then goes on to add, "If a man love Me, he will keep My Word; and My Father will love Him, and I will love him, and I will manifest Myself unto him, and We will come unto him AND MAKE OUR ABODE WITH HIM." And then, at the close of the High Priestly prayer, He asks, "That

the love wherewith Thou lovest Me may be in them, and I
IN THEM." Is it not evident that our Lord speaks here of
something far beyond the initial grace of pardon and regenera-
tion? He speaks of what would be given to those who love
Him and keep His commandments; of something that would
be the special gift of the Holy Ghost dwelling and working in
them. Even so Paul, in speaking of his prayer, that God
would, according to the riches of His glory, do something
special and "mightily strengthen their inner man," and then
in his doxology, giving glory to God, as "able to do something exceeding abundantly above what we ever could ask
or think," would have us feel that the blessing he holds out
to us is that in which the spiritual life culminates as the highest
exhibition of what the mighty power of God can work in us.

Christ dwelling in the heart. Let us begin where Paul
begins, "I bow my knees," and in urgent prayer for ourselves,
and for God's children around us, plead with God to do something according to the riches of His glory, which will lift
us out of our feebleness, and bring us into the life that will
be to the praise of His glory.

2. The connection between being strengthened by the
Spirit and having Christ in the heart is brought out with
great beauty in a sketch of the life of Miss E. Duncan, to be
found in chapter xv of the volume on *The Christ-life*, by Rev.
J. B. Figgis. In a letter giving an account of her experience
she writes: "I must write you to help me to magnify the Lord.
He has been coming into my soul this past week as never
before, and I am feeling most blessedly possessed with Him.
For months the cry of my heart has been to be filled, and
every week the longing grew intenser; not for joy—it was
Himself, HIMSELF, that is what I wanted. I had been longing
and praying for this fulness of the Spirit, and yet I did ask the
Lord to keep me waiting for a thorough preparation. He kept
me waiting for months, but all that time I was waiting on the
Lord and crying after the blessing with tears. I am sure that
is the right way to do when He keeps us waiting. On Sunday
evening last He came and has taken full possession. I do not
know how to express my experience, for I seem to have lost
all sense of experience in the sublime reality of His continual presence. When I could say I wanted neither happiness

nor usefulness, but Jesus only, then the Beloved Bridegroom came back, and I am perfectly satisfied with HIM. I have God, and I want no more. Self has been subdued by the King reigning triumphantly. I see I have been erring, and fancying I had a stock of grace within, instead of not only realising that I am nothing, but also that I HAVE nothing, that Jesus has it all for me."

In letters to friends she speaks of experiencing to the very depths the truths concerning the fulness of the Spirit. To one she writes: "Tell her not to rest until she is FILLED with the Spirit." To another, "Trust fully, follow fully; keep on trusting for the fulness of the blessing." To her fellow-teachers, "May I give you a parting message,—a very great author says, 'Be filled with the Spirit'. Are you? Do you realise the tremendous blessing that will come to you, from you, if you are?"

In spite of the promise that the living water shall be in us springing up perpetually, many doubt the maintenance of such a life. But He who gave can keep. "One cannot LIVE upon the mountain tops," a minister said to her. "I HAVE lived upon them for months," she said. And those were months of suffering even to agony. It would be easy to multiply expressions of her absolute trust in God, and easy in uttering them to every one thus upon the hill-top, but are we willing to climb? She was never weary of urging all she loved to seek to be filled with the Spirit, assured that His blessings were for them as much as for her. To one friend she sent the message: "God can satisfy her fully every moment; He satisfied ME for months with Himself only." To another: "My earnest desire is that she may be filled with the Spirit, and then she will know what it is to be shut up to Christ." Elsewhere she says, "I used to pray: Lord, make me holy at all costs—with agony of body or mind if nothing else will do. And God took me at my word. I cannot tell you what joy it gives me that I consecrated all fully to the Lord. Tell every Christian it is worth while."

All this happiness was not for herself. As the working time grew shorter God let her have a glimpse of His view of the lost—some share of sympathy with Jesus about them. When cut off from pleading with others she would plead for them—

"plead all night if she had strength, and always with such certainty of being answered." Some one had suggested that she might expect some special blessing after special suffering. "I said, 'May I, Lord?' and the answer came, 'Yes, my child.' 'Then, Oh! give me the spirit of intercession,' and it came so strong at once."

Perhaps the difference between the state of fulness of blessing and that which preceded, may be manifested most by an extract, in which she says, "My besetting sin was pride: I know it was; and though I prayed to God for deliverance over and over again, I never got the mastery over it till I received the fulness of the Spirit. I DID like praise, and you know I had plenty of it; but now when people praise me it does not seem to touch me—it falls off me like water off a dyke. I just feel I am sin—sin, nothing else, and every scrap of good in me is all of God, and I want every one to think so too."

And this leads me to the last trait of character on which I would enlarge, and on which I want to lay stress. The sense that the grace manifested in her, and the glory seen upon her, were not hers, but GIVEN. In a deeply touching conversation, one of her doctors, speaking of the other, said, "Ah, he feels just as I do—not good, like you, but wicked." "Do you think me good?" "I do." "But I am not. We are just exactly alike—both poor sinners; but here lies the difference, what you see in me, and think good, is not me; it is not Emmeline Duncan, but the beautiful robe that Christ has put on me, and what you like is not me, but Christ, and He wants to clothe you with this robe too. Will you promise me to pray constantly—'Reveal Thyself to me, show me Thyself'? Just go into your room by yourself and speak to Him. He will save you; I know He will; and will not that be nice, and to bring others too?"

No wonder she could speak of the overwhelming sense of conscious union with Jesus.

CHAPTER XVII

See *The Alps of the New Testament: A Study in Ephesians*, by Miss A. P. Ferguson. Huguenot College, Wellington (Maskew Miller, Cape Town.)